Issues of War

Published by
Luviri Press
P/Bag 201 Luwinga
Mzuzu 2
Malawi

ISBN 978-99960-60-22-9
e ISBN 978-99960-60-59-5

Luviri Press is represented outside Africa by:
African Books Collective Oxford (order@africanbookscollective.com)

www.mzunipress.blogspot.com

www.africanbookscollective.com

editorial assistance and cover: Daniel Neumann

Printed in Malawi by Baptist Publications, P.O. Box 444, Lilongwe

Issues of War

Fr Rodney Schofield

Luviri Press

Mzuzu

2018

St Ambrose' Church, Wye

LENT 2015

ISSUES OF WAR
with Fr Rodney

Tuesdays 11am - 12 noon
24 February
3, 10, 17 March

The pity of war
War in the Hebrew tradition
Christian thinking about war
Propaganda and dissent

Content

Here we have no lasting city, but we seek the city which is to come

Introduction

The term 'war' is an evolving concept. Whereas it may once have evoked images of armed men attacking each other in tribal disputes or in larger-scale operations launched by national leaders, it has since branched out into many more varieties such as 'economic' war, 'guerrilla' war, 'civil' war, 'cyber' war – any or all of which may now accompany conventional types of fighting. Alongside these lurks the terrifying possibility of 'nuclear' war – yet even 'cyber' war which is conducted over the internet and fires no grenades or rockets can have consequences that are almost as devastating.

The reflections that follow (offered at St Ambrose' Catholic Church in Wye, Kent during Lent 2015 during the centenary of World War 1) do not cover nearly such a wide spectrum, but focus on what is perhaps best described as 'armed conflict'. It is clear that, whereas in past centuries Christian thought was much concerned to constrain such hostilities, for example by limiting them to defensive needs and outlawing abuse of non-combatants, it has become increasingly necessary to promote peace and justice as the prime means of resolving conflict and building a more stable world. This was certainly emphasised in the conciliar documents of Vatican 2, and remains paramount in Catholic thinking.

In the world today there is abundant evidence that, although there continues to be much international unease, armed conflict now occurs far more commonly within particular countries (or regions) rather than as a means of settling disputes between states. One consequence of this development has been the huge number of civilian casualties and the flow of refugees across borders. This has given rise to the recent concept of 'humanitarian intervention'. This continues to be clarified since there is otherwise room for it to be invoked too readily as a pretext for foreign invasion, where in reality the motivation may well be self-interest (e.g. to protect oil supplies) or ideological hostility (e.g. against communism or Islam) rather than compassion for the victims of violence. Here the churches' response has tended to focus on aid relief rather than on the merits or otherwise of military action.

Thus, whereas Christian thought once carried much international weight and undoubtedly dampened the human instinct for self-preservation and revenge, today it is mainly secular bodies such as the United Nations that provide some restraint upon individual governments. This of course is limited, since it is perfectly possible for world opinion to be ignored. Church leaders need nevertheless to influence such opinion by appealing to universal human values and to the widespread efforts of Christians to regenerate human societies. Although politicians are sometimes critical of church 'intervention' in public affairs, Christians have always prayed for God's kingdom to come on earth – and this can never be limited to the sphere of personal devotion: Christ's kingship may not be 'of this world' [John 18.36] but there are no aspects of human life where his example and his teaching are irrelevant.

Because the Church in its different manifestations is present in so many varied situations, it can sometimes articulate the sufferings and pain of those who have no one else to speak for them. So alongside such wisdom as it has inherited through its scriptures and its historic debates, it can still today be a voice for those who bear the brunt of war. It can remind us too that it is often poets, or artists, or dramatists who express the truth most clearly. Since war in the end affects the entire world, peace is a project to engage us all.

1. The Pity of War

The centenary of the 1st World War (1914 – 1918) has been widely commemorated in recent years. Given that many more wars have since broken out in the world, and that horrors and tragedies on an unimaginable scale continue to happen, it is surely important that such commemorations should not only recall (for example) what life was like in the trenches, what sacrifices were made and how many lives were lost, perhaps too the difficulties faced by those who remained at home, but should also include serious reflection on the reasons why hostilities broke out when they did, and some assessment of what in the end was really achieved. The focus, however, seems to have been much more upon the progress and conduct of that 'war to end all wars' than upon any analysis of its causes and its lasting effects. The impression given is that it is generally found much easier to salute bravery and heroism than to think about the morality and conduct of warfare, the wisdom or otherwise of politicians, and the far-reaching consequences for individuals, for the economy, for world affairs and so on – those big issues that continue to haunt us. But some people have thought about these things, and so here I want to introduce a few of the important contributions that artists, poets, dramatists, novelists and indeed historians have offered both in ancient times and more recently. They have been much readier than politicians to face the stark reality of war, to tell the truth about it and to learn lessons from it. They make an excellent antidote to the all-too-common jingoism – 'my country right or wrong' – that the media too frequently serve up for us. It was particularly refreshing (to give just one initial illustration) to hear the Scottish historian Neil Ferguson commenting on WW1: 'We rushed into that war,' he said, 'to resist German expansionism and to protect our empire.' 50 years later, he pointed out, our empire had gone, and 100 years later it was quite obvious that Angela Merkel's dominance of Europe far exceeded the miniscule support for David Cameron. (In parenthesis, isn't it rather odd that in 1701 the Westminster Parliament passed an Act of Settlement which declared Sophia of Hanover to be the heiress presumptive to Queen Anne, so that in 1714 her eldest son George, the Elector of Hanover, became King of England? The line of thinking, of course, was that anyone's better than a Roman Catholic – even a German!)

So, what was the point of all those millions slaughtered then? At the time, you weren't supposed to mention them. Perhaps the most famous case is that of the British artist C.R.W.Nevinson. He features, very commendably, in an exhibition called *Truth and Memory: British Art of the First World War* which was held at the Imperial War Museum in London for several months in 2014-15. The irony is that they wouldn't have hung his painting *Paths of Glory* (1918) a hundred years ago. It depicts dead soldiers, and when the Ministry of Information censored such realism Nevinson simply put a banner across it that read 'censored' and kept it on display at the Leicester Galleries in London. They then charged him with 'unauthorised use of the word *censored*'.

Nevinson was certainly not the first war artist to be treated in this way. Forty years earlier (in 1874) two paintings by the Russian Vasily Vereshchagin were similarly turned down for a St Petersburg exhibition. *Left Behind*, which depicted a dying soldier deserted by his fellows, along with *The Apotheosis of War*, dedicated 'to all conquerors, past, present and to come' as a stark reminder of its bleak consequences, were denied a showing on the grounds that they portrayed the Russian military in a poor light!

Commenting on another of Nevinson's pictures (*La Mitrailleuse*) at the time, an art critic wrote in the *London Evening News* that 'when war is no more, this picture will stand, to the astonishment and shame of our descendants, as an example of what civilised

man did to civilised man in the first quarter of the twentieth century'. The problem of course was that the weaponry of war had unleashed destructive powers unknown to previous generations, so that not only were soldiers killed in larger numbers but – crucially – their colleagues were wounded and mutilated so badly that nearly a quarter of a million needed amputations quite apart from the tens of thousands who suffered head or eye injuries.

The reality of modern 'industrial' warfare was certainly not anticipated by the public at large (and probably not by many of the politicians). Diaries written in 1914 (whether in England, France, Germany or Russia) betray a naive optimism that the fighting would be over within a month or two, and victory would be easily won by the writer's own nation. When British forces retreated from superior German numbers that August at the Battle of Mons, reporters from *The Times* gave a sobering account: their potentially demoralising report led to the immediate exclusion of journalists

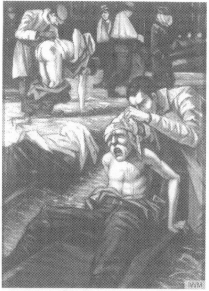

from the frontline. The government needed to portray their troops as indestructible and invincible, and their war as the inevitable triumph of good over evil.

Nevinson was not himself a pacifist; he believed in the cause for which Britain was fighting, but wanted to express the truth about the horrors and (in his words) 'the so-called sacrifice' of war. 'I had seen sights so revolting that man seldom conceives of them in his.' Thus he spoke for the many privates and a few officers who were 'to all purposes inarticulate'. It seemed to him that 'the war-mongers of the world' had a monopoly. So in an earlier painting, *The Doctor* (1916) - seen here on page 11 - his interpretation of 'sacrifice' banishes its customary redemptive overtones: behind the soldier in the foreground is a meaningless corpse – a fully bandaged figure (a dead soldier) has been abandoned.

His picture challenges the deceitful message conveyed by those that appeared earlier in the war, such as James Clark's famous *The Great Sacrifice*. An army chaplain, Geoffrey Gordon, wrote in 1917: 'You remember the picture of the Great Sacrifice.... Like the young lad in the picture, the man whom I saw die had a bullet wound in the temple, but there the likeness ceased. Here was no calm death, but a ghastly mess of blood and brains and mud, on his face and in the surrounding trench; and in the stark horror of the moment I could not see the Crucified at all.'

Nevinson justified his paintings by insisting that he didn't portray 'horror' but 'reality'. Even so, it was but a partial reality. No doubt there was much less opportunity to paint dead or mutilated Germans (although they were photographed for the archives), but today it is only jihadists who display their victims to the world. The British public is allowed to mourn the loss of kith and kin but any casualties inflicted (unless incurred by prominent military personnel) are sanitised. Those responsible for the gruesome operation of war use disingenuous metaphors: 'shooting and bombing' is termed *kinetic activity*; 'kidnap and torture' is *extraordinary rendition*; 'slaughtered civilians' are mere *collateral damage*, while their homes are impersonal *compounds*; the enemy is not 'killed' but *neutralised*. It is emphatically the home team who suffers; what happens to others is euphemistically glossed over.

Indeed, during the course of WW1 it was politically correct to picture German soldiers as sub-human, mere animals. Thus, in 1916 a propaganda poster by the Belgian artist Gisbert Combaz was headed *Kochonneries*, meaning 'junk food' (from the word for a pig). It showed fat troopers in a charcuterie, and (to avoid any doubt) spelt its title with a Germanic K instead of the correct French C. Its aim was to encourage such 'rubbish' people to be hung up like the meat on which they gorged.

Yet, leaving aside the combatants, there were other victims of modern warfare's destructiveness – and some artists were only too aware of this. One of Nevinson's contemporaries was Paul Nash, whose earlier paintings often celebrated the natural world. By 1918, however, he found that much of the country-side had been devastated. In his painting *We are making a New World* the trees are shown blasted to pieces in a landscape of mud and shell craters.

Similar 'wastelands' are found in other commissions that Nash executed at the end of the war. *The Menin Road* depicts a maze of flooded trenches and shell craters while tree stumps, devoid of any

13

foliage, point towards a sky full of clouds and plumes of smoke bisected by shafts of sunlight resembling gun barrels. Two soldiers attempting to follow the road are lost in unrecognisable surroundings.

The Wire shows more starkly a tree trunk wrapped in barbed wire. The artist described himself (in a letter to his wife) as 'a messenger' from the front-line: 'I am no longer an artist interested and curious, I am a messenger who will bring back word from the men who are fighting to those who want the war to go on for ever (*once started it is very hard indeed to stop a war*). Feeble, inarticulate, will be my message, but it will have a bitter truth, and may it burn their lousy souls.'

More shocking than those so far mentioned are some of the pictures produced by the portraitist William Orpen who was commissioned to paint what was presumably hoped would be an inspiring record of courageous troops. Instead he saw abandoned battle-fields and rotting flesh, and called one of his portraits *Blown Up – Mad.* When he used similarly emaciated, half-naked figures against a coffin draped in the Union Jack the War Museum refused to accept it ('it does not show what we wished shown') until the offending figures were painted out: the picture was labelled *To the Unknown Soldier in France.* He himself recorded that 'war's only tangible result is the ragged unemployed soldier and the dead'.

In the recent exhibition at the War Museum there was also a large canvas by John Singer Sargent. As an American artist he'd been asked late in the war to contribute something that reflected Anglo-American cooperation. What they got was this work called *Gassed*, which depicts the aftermath of a mustard gas attack. Helpless figures stagger along in single file with their bandaged eyes and hands on each other's shoulder. In the distance, beyond a scattering of dead bodies can be seen what might well be a mirage, a football match in progress.

Sargent seems to be deliberately reminding us here of the famous painting of 1568 by Pieter Bruegel the Elder entitled *'The Blind Leading the Blind'.* (There were those who considered that in the First World War it was a case of 'lions led by donkeys.')

Clearly there are reminiscences too of the paintings that emerged a hundred years before WW1 as a result of the struggle in Spain against the Napoleonic invaders. Francisco Goya is famous for his depictions of the horror and brutality experienced then. Goya's prints, published after his death under the title *The Disasters of War*, highlight the cruelty of the French forces and the fury of the Spanish people. Everyone involved appears to be dehumanised. The top picture concludes despairingly that 'nothing can be done'. The lower picture bears the title *Enterrar y callar*, meaning 'bury them and keep quiet'. Some panels mention 'wild beasts' – yet these are not soldiers, just frantic women trying to defend themselves and their children.

Goya intended that the truth should be seen even by 'those who have no wish to see it'. Similarly, when civil war broke out in Spain two decades after WW1 had ended, another Spanish artist Pablo Picasso reacted to the atrocities he saw being committed by painting his famous *Guernica* (1937).

Unlike Goya's prints this was not hidden from the public gaze but went on a world tour to great acclaim, helping to focus media attention upon what was taking place.

Such 'dehumanisation' is no rarity and brings us back again to the Great War, in particular to a deeper understanding of the phenomenon of 'shell-shock'. Perhaps the bewildered soldiers in Nash's *The Menin Road* are exhibiting early signs of it? On the 90th anniversary of the ending of WW1 (i.e. in 2008), Salisbury Playhouse staged a dramatisation of J.L.Carr's 1980 novel entitled *A Month in the Country*. It features two traumatised survivors of the war coming in the beautiful summer of 1920 to the Yorkshire village of Oxgodby. The hero, Tom Birkin, is there to uncover a medieval wall painting of the Last Judgement in the parish church. Thanks to shell-shock, he stammers violently and has a violent facial twitch, typical of men who had bayoneted others in the head. Working in a nearby field is Charles Moon, an archaeologist back from the trenches with a leg full of shrapnel. What the book and the play trace is the slow revival of the primeval rhythms of life so cruelly disorientated by the inhuman and unnatural theatre of war – and suggest, as psychiatrists gradually came to realise themselves, that shell-shock (of which at least 80,000 cases are recorded from WW1) is not simply a mental disturbance induced by the relentless noise of exploding artillery, but much more profoundly a spiritual recoil from exposure to bestial behaviour. Among the pioneers in treatment was William Rivers, 'a wonderful man' as one of his renowned patients Siegfried Sassoon later described him in his memoir *Sherston's Progress*. One of his supporters was Ernest Jones, President of the British Psycho-Analytic Association, who commented in 1917 that war constituted 'an official abrogation of civilised standards' – or in Sassoon's words an 'outraging' of humanity, even if 'sanctioned and glorified by the Church'.

'Natural Sciences, May 1914' Rivers second from left in bottom row.

The Fellow

Made famous by his representation in the *Regeneration* trilogy by Pat Barker, William Halse Rivers Rivers, is one of the most important figures in the field of psychology. His association with the University began in 1893 with a lectureship on the Physiology of the Sense Organs, establishing a relationship with St John's that was to last 29 years. His arrival at the College was met with some hostility because of the position he had been offered and the subject of psychophysics. Despite this, Rivers launched himself into the life of the College and spent much of his time here.

Rivers was in Australia when war broke out, and was unable to return to England until March 1915. He was determined to do something for the war effort, but was designated unfit for duty at the Front due to ill health. However, he discovered that the government was appealing for doctors to work with soldiers with psychological damage and shellshock, and he was appointed to work at Maghull Hospital in Liverpool. It was here that Rivers' Talking Cure, a method still used in the treatment of trauma illness, began to emerge. His own experiences taught him that he needed to get to know each of his patients as individuals, and treat them as such, because since each man's experience would be unique, so his 'cure' should be. It is at this point that Rivers was sent to Scotland, to Craiglockhart Hospital for Officers, where he was to spend the rest of the war. He soon became caught up in a running battle with the government, who did not accept that shellshock was a genuine psychological problem for the soldiers, and who objected to Rivers' methods of treatment. It is a measure of how well-regarded Rivers was by the College, that in 1919 a new position was created for him: Praelector of Natural Science Studies. Rivers died suddenly on 4 June 1922, but his influence in the fields of neurology and psychology ensured his legacy to the medical profession.

Before Rivers (whose long association with St John's College, Cambridge is recorded above) delved further, even the most sympathetic hospitalisation had usually failed to plumb the depths of the problem, assuming that time out from the front would fairly readily get soldiers back on their feet again. (The less sympathetic view was that the condition was 'put on' by malingerers.) The war-damaged Siegfried Sassoon expressed suitable scepticism in his poem *Survivors*:

No doubt they'll soon get well; the shock and strain
Have caused their stammering, disconnected talk.
Of course they're 'longing to go out again', -
These boys with old, scared faces, learning to walk.
They'll soon forget their haunted nights; their cowed
Subjection to the ghosts of friends who died, -
Their dreams that drip with murder; and they'll be proud
Of glorious war that shatter'd all their pride ...
Men who went out to battle, grim and glad;
Children, with eyes that hate you, broken and mad.

What was actually needed was well expressed by Michael Tippett in his much later oratorio *A Child of Our Time.* He wrote this in the early years of the 2nd World War, inspired by an incident in Paris in 1938. A young Polish Jew whose family had been arrested by the Gestapo was being sheltered illegally in France by his uncle; he shot and killed a German diplomat, and although he was then imprisoned by the French authorities, the Nazis launched their notoriously savage Kristallnacht by way of reprisal. While the libretto narrates these events, its central theme is the need for all of us to come to terms with our own evil side – without projecting it on to an enemy. Towards the end, a tenor followed by the whole choir sings the words 'I would know my shadow and my light, so shall I at last be whole.'

Soldiers returning from Iraq and Afghanistan have much the same inner turmoil to cope with today. Of course, there are also highly commendable qualities exhibited in such extreme conditions – bravery, loyalty to one's comrades, even the readiness for self-sacrifice – but the daily context is totally abnormal, to the extent that the lives of innocent civilians, including women and children, can be readily obliterated in the pursuit of military objectives. As Catholic chaplain at RNAS Yeovilton, the naval air station, I recall conversations with intelligent and highly devout Catholic officers who were all too ready to write off such casualties, even if numbered by the thousand, as a necessary but none the less 'trivial' side-effect of targeted bombardment. Yet if they had seen the dead bodies and devastation at close hand for themselves, I doubt if their consciences would have left them so unconcerned and stony-hearted. The operation of long-range weapons and drones may release combatants from the effects of shell-induced shock, but if so, it must surely mean an escalation of inhumanity.

This takes us to a more recent artist and another exhibition, namely, *Shock and Awe* held late last summer in Bristol at the Royal West of England Academy. This, according to the gallery's website, was 'an exhibition of work by contemporary artists recently exposed to the front-line of war in Iraq, Afghanistan and the Balkans' – and also 'a platform for artists who are fascinated by acts of remembrance, who use their art as a warning, as a form of protest at the wickedness of the world'. The one who should particularly interest us is, I think, Jill Gibbon. Working largely undercover and through the guise of taking down notes, she managed to sketch images of the surreal and entirely callous behind-the-scenes world of military fairs and expos. These highlight for us how the arms trade treats missiles, tanks and bombs like any other commodity. So at arms fairs in London and Paris, buyers eye up a range of tanks, helicopters, designer drones and branded bombs, while scantily clad women drape themselves over racks of missiles, reminiscent of the 'booth babes' at tech conventions or at the launch of new luxury cars. Her motives are both aesthetic and political. 'I think arms fairs give an insight into the way weapons are treated as commodities by the arms trade,' she says. 'The wine, pretzels and gifts, the saleswomen leaning against tanks, give the impression that weapons are simply objects of exchange. There is little sign of their destructive effects.'

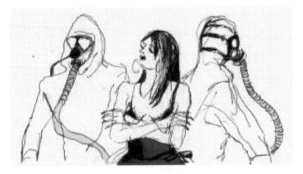

'In this drunken, heady world' she adds, 'a weapon is just a product, and a repressive regime another client.'

There are reminiscences here of David Jones' classic account of his WW1 experiences *In Parenthesis* (1937): He records how his adjutant introduced the Mills bomb which scattered shrapnel far and wide and then 'sauntered off with his sections of grenades and fuses and explanatory diagrams of their mechanisms stuffed into the pockets of his raincoat, like a departing commercial traveller.' The analogy is not entirely unfair, given that between 1914 and 1918 the British Army bought around 5 million tons of shells alone, quite apart from other weaponry, which no doubt brought very considerable profits to those who made them. Prior to the commencement of hostilities, it appears that technical know-how about the development of armaments was not always a closely guarded secret: Britain, France, Germany and Russia sometimes pooled their expertise, mutually intensifying the future horror of war.

About ten years prior to the ministry I undertook at Yeovilton, I recall a debate in General Synod on land mines. You may remember this issue had been highlighted by Princess Di because of their terrible long term impact.

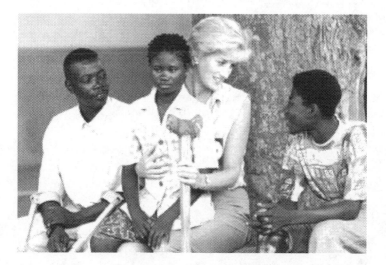

Years after the ending of conflict agricultural workers (which often means women and children) can come across these unexploded bombs and be blown to smithereens by accidentally triggering them off. The campaign was in full swing to outlaw their use right across the world, and synod was then trying to give moral support to the British government to endorse any international agreements. All was going well until a private member, I think from Gloucester diocese, stood up and opposed the motion on the grounds that, if the measure went through, some fifteen hundred workers near where he lived would be without a job. He rejected the call for a safer and more peaceable world in favour of local employment opportunities.

In essence, our government continues to back the same principle by its massive support for the arms trade – which includes turning a blind eye to much bribery and corruption, since sales are worth nearly £40 billion a year. The trade was highlighted last year when Ukraine first came into the headlines: at the same time as condemning the Russians for their collusion with rebels, the annual flow of weapons to them (valued at several million pounds) was not seriously questioned. Nor does Britain give much consideration to the way some of our traded weapons end up in irresponsible hands, allowing them to be used against us or to fuel conflicts around the world. In other words, we do not seem to have sufficiently joined up policies, or a coherent ethic that can respond adequately to the many lobbying interested parties. And sadly too, whistle-blowers in the industry who expose some of the huge back-handers are extremely vulnerable to personal sanctions.

One other recent exhibition offers food for thought, not so much on the brutality of war, nor on the profits that can be made from it, but on its wider lasting impact. *Flesh and Bone* was held at the Ashmolean Museum in Oxford rather more than a year ago and brought together two major artists of the 20th century, Francis Bacon and Henry Moore. Moore first came to fame in the 1940s as a war artist, particularly with pictures of women and children sheltering from the Blitz on the platforms of the London Underground, and he evokes the apprehension and uncertainty hanging over them. When they emerge, if they emerge, who and what will have been destroyed? What makes the pictures timeless is that we share similar fears today – the future of our world seems increasingly uncertain, as insecurities continue to emerge in bewildering variety.

This is reflected too in Bacon's 1952 painting *Man kneeling in Grass*: a nude figure is on all fours apparently eating grass, spied upon us who in turn – so the lurking shadows in the picture suggest – are spied on by other unseen observers in the process. It dates from an era when nuclear war was the greatest threat. A novel written towards the end of that era also speculates what the world might be like in its aftermath: *Riddley Walker* (1980) by the American writer Russell Hoban is actually set in East Kent (with familiar places renamed e.g. Wye itself is known as How). Life has regressed and technology, 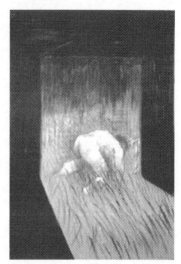 such as it is, is back to the Iron Age. So we wonder: will we too one day be stripped of what we have and reduced to eating grass (like king Nebuchadnezzar in the book of Daniel) – or will we have to shelter in primitive stockades and be forced to feed on wild animals (and perhaps in their absence to eat our own children)? Even if today we dismiss such alarming scenarios as mere flights of fancy, we are constantly reminded of the many malevolent agencies who threaten to wreak global forms of destruction.

It is instructive to observe recent artists and writers gaining important insights from medieval or classical resources. Russell Hoban was stimulated by a mural in Canterbury Cathedral, the 15th century *Legend of St Eustace*: it helped him to realise that our modern idea of progress is but a delusion. In the exhibition just mentioned Henry Moore (perhaps influenced by Owen's poem of 1917 *The Fates*) incorporated the three

Greek Fates, 'the daughters of Necessity' who are described in Plato's *Republic* by a man called Er who although left for dead on the battlefield later revived and reported his glimpses into the world beyond, namely: Clotho who spins the thread of each person's life, Lachesis who measures its length, and Atropos who severs it. These characters appear in two of Moore's air raid shelter paintings, when the cutting short of people's lives was very much in the air. Here, on the right of *Four Figures in a Setting* (1948), Atropos is hidden behind a blood-soaked screen from the others: so the person sheltering on the far left has no means of telling what lies ahead, whether for himself or the world in general.

Francis Bacon on the other hand featured the three Furies whose role is far more terrifying: the ancient law of the Furies required blood to be paid for with blood in an unending cycle of vengeance, so their inclusion begs the question, Will war ever end? Are we doomed to be steeped in a perpetual bloodbath?

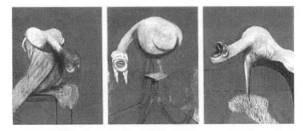

The Greek dramatist Aeschylus was optimistic when he wrote the *Oresteia* (which features the Furies) in the aftermath of the long-drawn out wars with the Persians. His work seems to affirm that there is ultimately a more civilised way to live, and to engage with others, than to be ruled by our basic instincts. So for him the Furies become Eumenides, the kindly ones, the guardian spirits of Athens. If such a transformation was never fully realised, at least we are reminded that centuries ago

24

people were already grappling with issues similar to those we face ourselves.

The poets and dramatists of the past are therefore still worthy of our attention. In the 5th century BC drama was staged in public arenas as much to address these debates as to entertain the masses. Greece at that time was not a unified country but a collection of independent city states, sometimes held together in alliance (which is how the Persians were defeated) but sometimes warring against each other. There was a particular rivalry between Athens and Sparta, especially after Athens began to demand tribute from other cities and to create a small empire of its own. Yet Athens was also the pioneer of democracy, particularly through the promotion of plays. These were staged in the open air theatre and often explored the tragic consequences of mistaken civic policies; in time they came to lampoon some of those who held public office. In effect they opened wide the opportunity for serious public debate about the issues of the day, and what should be done. Most of the dramatists knew from their own experience what war was like, so Aeschylus who fought in the battle of Marathon had no illusions about the horror of war. One of his greatest plays is *The Persians*, the story of how Athens' enemy responded to their defeat at the crucial sea-battle of Salamis. In the end the Persian king Darius returns as a ghost and tells those who've survived that it was their hubris that ultimately destroyed them. The point of course is that this is Aeschylus' warning to his fellow Athenians: 'Go carefully, avoid doing what the Persians did, don't attempt to subjugate others.'

Whereas, however, conflict and violent confrontation can arise in any situation fairly spontaneously, the waging of war usually depends upon the deliberate decision of political leaders. We know that when a million or more marched through London to avert military action against Saddam Hussein's Iraq, the Prime Minister Tony Blair was oblivious to their pleas. Too often in recent years our own national leaders have intervened in the affairs of other countries without adequately thinking what the long term consequences might be. Power and pride and the desire to be seen strutting on the world stage seem to have gone to their heads.

ANTI-WAR PROTESTS (estimated figures)

| New York 100,000 | London 1 million | Barcelona 1.3million |
| Rome 1 million |
| Baghdad 1 million |
| Calcutta 10,000 |
| San Francisco 200,000 | Damascus 200,000 | Sydney 200,000 |

Seminarians in Malawi asked me at the time if I thought the war on Iraq was right. I suggested that – though it might take much longer – lasting solutions were usually homegrown rather than imposed from outside.

Among the Athenian dramatists Sophocles was even more forceful in making this point than Aeschylus. In his play *Antigone*, which was staged at the Gulbenkian Theatre in Canterbury last autumn, the villain is Creon, king of Thebes, who after seizing power refuses to listen to those around him and condemns Antigone to be buried alive in a cave for her persistent attempts to give her brother a decent burial. Others are caught up in the plot: Haemon (Creon's son) who's betrothed to Antigone stands by her, and commits suicide; when Eurydice who is Creon's wife hears of his death she too kills herself. All this has been predicted by Tiresias, the prophet who although blind sees far more clearly into the future than Creon, who's blinded by his dictatorial pride and his inability to hear and understand what others are saying. *Antigone* may appear to be just a domestic tragedy, but the audience well understands that the play is a critique of 'realpolitik'.

Athens, alas, never learnt the lesson. Later in the 5th century as they vied for power with Sparta they demanded active support in their struggle from other cities within their sphere of influence. Melos refused, insisting that they were neutral. As a result Athenian ships were sent, Melos was invaded and their citizens were either slaughtered or enslaved. The following

MR. IMPORTANT

year Euripides presented his play *Trojan Women*, not ostensibly about Athens at all since it showed on the stage what had been done centuries earlier by the Greeks when they captured Troy. But it displayed their barbarism, with the audience well able to make the implied connections with more recent events. If now Athenians themselves had behaved inhumanely, they too would reap the consequences. Thus, the common message of these three great dramatists is that those who overreach themselves and inflict the horrors of war on others will soon find that the turn of events is well beyond their control. We might ask ourselves, Have we yet learnt that lesson?

Thus far, I have made no appeal to biblical sources or to Christian teaching. We shall engage more fully with these in due course. But reflections that are not altogether dissimilar from the classic Greek dramas do appear in the Bible. They emerged at much the same time because of the calamitous events that overtook the Jewish people, namely, their invasion by foreign powers and their eventual deportation into exile in the 6th century BC.

We are familiar with the earlier and highly exaggerated rhetoric of the Israelites themselves conquering the so-called Promised Land and attempting to annihilate the already settled tribes who stood in their way; but any unfettered occupation they enjoyed did not in fact last for more than a few centuries. So what went wrong? This was the question that pre-occupied the scribes who, during the years of exile and afterwards, shaped the final version of many Old Testament texts. The Jewish classification of their scriptures – as we know from several New Testament works – was to divide them into the Law, the Prophets and the Writings. Pre-eminence was given to the Law, that is the Torah; but there is much theology also in the so-called Prophets, which actually incorporate what we know as the historical books (but termed the Former Prophets). The Writings for the most part came a little later, after the time we're now considering, which is the 5th and 6th centuries BC. It is now recognised that the historical works, such as 1 and 2 Samuel, 1 and 2 Kings, are not impartial, carefully researched accounts of the centuries leading up to the Babylonian conquest, but a highlighting of 'significant' events. While they undoubtedly draw upon court annals and other 'factual' sources their genre is what might be called 'narrative theology'.

In particular, the setbacks experienced in the latter part of David's reign are seen against the weaknesses of David's own personality, and the editors (if we can use that term) indicate that this was typical of so many of Israel's leaders. What we read is not (as happens often elsewhere) a white-washing of the past, but an honest admission that God's plan for Israel is unlikely ever to become a reality because of the all too common character failings of her chief men. Abraham, Jacob, Moses had their faults, and because their human weakness is recognised, the Pentateuch ends on a very uncertain note – the Israelites are still outside the Promised Land. The question mark is there: if they do manage to invade and conquer and settle, will it be theirs for as long as they would hope?

The inclusion of David's domestic circumstances in the text suggests a deliberate attempt to pinpoint where (like the Greek rulers) he fell short, as did those who succeeded him. The opening verses of 2 Samuel 11 include ominous words:

> In the spring of the year, the time when kings go forth to battle, David sent Joab, and his servants with him, and all Israel; and they ravaged the Ammonites, and besieged Rabbah. But David remained at Jerusalem.

And in Jerusalem he was viewing Bathsheba in the process of bathing. To compound his absence from the war zone, he now summoned Uriah home from the front in the hope that any child he might have conceived with Bathsheba would be acknowledged as Uriah's. Uriah, however, kept his sacred battle vow and stayed away from Bathsheba – a fact which was reported to the king. He then arranged for Uriah to be placed in the very thick of the fighting, where sure enough he was killed.

A whole further chain of events then follows, and Nathan the prophet warns David of the consequences: 'The sword shall never depart from your house'. First, the baby born of David's union with Bathsheba dies in infancy. Then Amnon, one of David's offspring, seduces his

The letter that seals Uriah's fate

28

half sister Tamar. Her brother Absalom takes revenge and has Amnon slaughtered after getting him drunk. Soon afterwards he pits himself in revolt against his father David, who has to flee before finally mustering his troops. Eventually Absalom is slain on David's orders. Another rebellion occurs and then, after it has been suppressed, disaster strikes again in the form of a three year famine. As if this is not enough retribution from on high, the Philistines then resume attacks upon Israel. These are warded off, and in his last days David recalls God's goodness in a psalm of thanksgiving. Yet even now the editors have not said everything: the last chapter of 2 Samuel recounts David's earlier transgression in carrying out his own census of the people, instead of heeding what God's plan of action might be. This time his penitence is recorded, so the book ends: 'The Lord heeded supplications for the land, and the plague was averted from Israel'.

It seems however that a later generation of redactors was not over-impressed by this account – it seemed to let David off too lightly. In the version presented by the Chronicler it was truly his bloodlust that had overstepped the mark, and thus rendered him unfit for spiritual leadership:

> You have shed much blood and have waged great wars; you shall not build a house to my name, because you have shed so much blood before me upon the earth. [1 Chron 22.8]

One might easily imagine that the whole saga was composed by one of our Greek dramatists: the message is so similar, that a ruler's personal failings can ruin his country, that war and conflict follow greed and pride as certainly as night follows day.

There are narrative details in the gospels which also reflect how easily truth and justice are perverted by human corruption. Their climax is not the outbreak of war, but the officially sanctioned murder of an innocent man. Few come out of the story with any credit. The voice of the people is shown to be fickle, no doubt swayed by bribes or political threats. One day they shout 'Hosanna', and a mere five days later change it to 'Crucify him'. Jesus' supporters profess their loyalty and then desert him or deny knowing him. Jewish religious leaders distort his message and present him as a threat to the country's stability; in fact, his only challenge is to their own teaching and status. The Roman governor washes his hands of the problem, and sentences him to death for the sake of expediency with a blind disregard for the truth. The whole episode is a paradigm of how vested interests combine to produce catastrophic outcomes.

It is J.M.W.Turner who, in one of his more enigmatic paintings *Pilate washes his Hands* (1830), presents the confusion and complexity of the situation. To our surprise he places Mary in the centre of the picture. Why? because she, unlike Pilate (who stands left of her with his back to us clutching a towel), is looking up in search of divine guidance. We then realise that Pilate has actually turned his back, not just on us who view the picture, but on God. There is a huge crowd in the background, who are scarcely illuminated at all. It is the young mother and child sitting in the foreground who are seen most distinctly. They may well represent Mary and Jesus at an earlier stage of life, but the implication is certainly that it is the innocent of heart who are closest to God and receptive of his truth and wisdom. Indeed, 'out of the mouth of babes and sucklings ...' were the very words of Jesus testifying to this a few days before his trial.

Tragically, however, we know it is they who will suffer, as did 'all the male children in Bethlehem and in all that region who were two years old or under' [Mt 2.16] at the time of Jesus' birth.

*   *   *   *   *   *   *   *   *

As we now proceed to examine some of the well-considered 'academic' arguments about the appropriate use of force, the circumstances in which the taking of life can be justified, the rights of self-defence, the meaning of a just war, and so on, it is important to bear these various pictures and stories in mind. They are needed to keep us in touch with reality. Indeed, even when people claim to be acting responsibly and reasonably, they may well be swayed by other factors too and may seldom have experienced for themselves the sort of misery, devastation and horror into which they plunge others.

Perhaps if our leaders today were prepared to learn from history, to heed the experience of others and to listen to contemporary warnings they might do better? In days gone by they might have consulted diviners (such as Tiresias) about future scenarios, but there is now much wisdom to be found elsewhere. It might not be a bad idea, for example, to heed the words of Pope Frances who has clearly set peace and reconciliation as one of the main objectives of his ministry, and through diplomacy rather than threats has already achieved a significant breakthrough in the relations between the USA and Cuba.

Odysseus consults Tiresias in the underworld:

Eurylochus (who in the end fatally disagrees) stands behind.

This calyx-krater (used for mixing wine and water) is dated about 380 BC.

It was found in 1964 and is attributed to the 'Dolon painter'. It is now kept in the Archaeological Museum, Zadar.

2. War in the Hebrew Tradition

One of the most disturbing aspects of the Old Testament is its account of Israel's forces going on the rampage to conduct indiscriminate slaughter of any settlement or tribe in Canaan who resisted them. Let me give one example:

> And the Lord said to Joshua, 'Do not fear or be dismayed; take all the fighting men with you, and arise, go up to Ai; see, I have given into your hand the king of Ai, and his people, his city, and his land; and you shall do to Ai and its king as you did to Jericho and its king; only its spoil and its cattle you shall take as booty for yourselves. [Josh 8.1-2]

And so they did. We read on:

> When Israel had finished slaughtering all the inhabitants of Ai in the open wilderness where they pursued them and all of them to the very last had fallen by the edge of the sword, all Israel returned to Ai, and smote it with the edge of the sword. And all who fell that day, both men and women, were twelve thousand, all the people of Ai. For Joshua did not draw back his hand, with which he stretched out the javelin, until he had utterly destroyed all the inhabitants of Ai. Only the cattle and the spoil of that city Israel took as their booty, according to the word of the LORD which he commanded Joshua. So Joshua burned Ai, and made it for ever a heap of ruins, as it is to this day. And he hanged the king of Ai on a tree until evening; and at the going down of the sun Joshua commanded, and they took his body down from the tree, and cast it at the entrance of the gate of the city, and raised over it a great heap of stones, which stands there to this day.

In other words, we have yet another episode of genocide, committed (so the text purports) at God's command. This followed a preliminary attack on Ai, which was rebuffed. Joshua's spies had misjudged the size and strength of the people there, so a much smaller force had been sent in initially, thirty-six of whom had been killed. You might well wonder if Ai was anywhere near the Gaza strip, but no – it was in the hill country to the north of Jerusalem, somewhere to the west of Jericho. Nor was there any claim that the men of Ai had started the quarrel by showering Joshua's troops with rocket attacks. This was an unprovoked attack which could scarcely be justified as self-defence. It was simply a land grab, supposedly because this particular tribe's legend was that one of their founding fathers (Abraham) had been told by God in a dream to go and get it: it was apparently his desire to have one nation and one country in the world where one religion alone would be practised.

Even though the traditional Christian reading is a spiritual one, in which those opposing Israel are taken symbolically to mean the sins within us and the temptations without, leaving passages like this for all and sundry to read for themselves is asking for trouble. It is not obvious from the text that what we are really required to do is to conduct a searching examination of our own souls and thereby discover what it is within each of us that is frustrating God's purposes. Nor does the text necessarily beckon us to understand it in the wider context of other biblical teachings about war and peace which may be less bloodthirsty. Literalists and fundamentalists too easily read themselves into the story, which will then justify their violent action against any who happen to be of a different race or religion. They are unlikely to ask the obvious question, Did these events really happen, or were they compiled at a later date as part of Israel's mythology, perhaps as an aetiological account of why various heaps of ancient stones dotted the landscape?

According to archaeologists, it is very uncertain whether Jericho was destroyed in Joshua's time – much depends upon the date ascribed to him as well as upon a more nuanced understanding of how Canaan came only gradually to be occupied by those who called themselves Israelites – or whether an earthquake was responsible.

Regardless of the historicity of such events, it is clear that over the centuries the Israelites saw a thread of divine involvement running through their fortunes both in time of war and in peacetime. Indeed, God himself is described as a warrior in what is apparently an ancient song of deliverance:

> The Lord is a man of war; the Lord is his name [Exod 15.3]

He is also referred to on a number of occasions as 'the Lord of hosts', which seems to suggest that he has his own heavenly armies to call upon. Divinely sanctioned fighting is certainly referred to time and again, but – given that biblical literature included much revision and editing as well as the addition of later writings – it is important to discern how ideas about war developed and changed over time.

Poussin – Joshua's Victory over the Amelekites 1625-6

War in the ancient Near East was in some respects a religious act, undertaken only after God himself had been consulted. I Kings 22 has a fascinating account of the kings of Israel and Judah trying to find out whether God would back them in a fight against Syria to regain some disputed territory. Four hundred prophets are summoned to discover God's will in the matter. No doubt after using various forms of divination, they all say the same thing:

> Go up; for the Lord will give it into the hand of the king. [v6]

But Jehoshaphat, king of Judah, is not convinced. So Ahab, king of Israel, sends for a character he doesn't particularly like, the prophet Micaiah. Sure enough, Micaiah parts company from the fawning yes-men, and predicts disaster. Ahab throws him into prison, and goes into battle regardless. As the reader has anticipated, he is shot through by an arrow and dies of his wounds.

However, an earlier example, in 1 Samuel 7, makes a telling contrast. When the people truly seek God's support, victory soon follows:

> As Samuel was offering up the burnt offering, the Philistines drew near to attack Israel; but the Lord thundered with a mighty voice that day against the Philistines and threw them into confusion; and they were routed before Israel. [v10]

So on this occasion God was an active participant in the battle, which was here a matter of self-defence. Even so, there were limits on the extent of retaliation spelt out in the principle of 'life for life, eye for eye, tooth for tooth, hand for hand, foot for foot, burn for burn, wound for wound, stripe for stripe [Exod 21.23-24]. In later terminology this would be described as a 'proportionate response' to aggression. So natural justice constrained the manner in which defensive wars might be fought.

Although the term 'wars of God' is seldom used [Num 21.14, 1 Sam 18.17, 25.28] it is arguable that the concept of a 'holy war' developed from tribal beginnings into a more sophisticated theological reformulation. Deuteronomy is the book that offers the most coherent account of it. Being written long after Israel had come to acquire the characteristics of a recognisable, organised state, it expresses the views of a later generation on the rationale for force. Despite its presentation as Moses' divinely informed teaching, it does not tell us how battles were in fact waged in or soon after Moses' own day and age, which was several centuries earlier. Rather, its exposition of the necessary use of military means, based on the lessons of history, is then read back into that history. Hence, it is more of a guide to what *should* have been done in the past than a realistic manual for the present.

What Deuteronomy clarifies most of all are the aims of a holy war. Two major themes emerge again and again. The *first* refers to the divinely promised possession of Israel's land. At the very beginning of the book, Moses specifies this as the main objective:

> Go in and take possession of the land which the Lord swore to your fathers, to Abraham, to Isaac, and to Jacob,   to give to them and to their descendants after them. [1.8]

There are a further nine reiterations of this promise that occur throughout Deuteronomy. Nevertheless, adjacent lands were specifically forbidden to the Israelites because these are detailed as God's gift to neighbouring peoples. This is very much in line with the evolving priestly understanding of clear-cut zones for most aspects of life, as expressed particularly in the later book Leviticus: there were distinctions between clean and unclean, the lay-out of the different temple courts (for men, for women, for priests and so on), the separation of meat and dairy products in kosher cooking, the ban on fabrics made of different types of material. In such thinking, there was little room for overlapping customs, beliefs, or racial affinities. In particular a *second* important theme is the need for the land of Israel to be made free of any false religion, especially any form of idolatry. Deuteronomy calls repeatedly for the destruction of any such practices and of those involved in them, although such purging is restricted to Israel's own territory:

> In the cities ... that the Lord your God gives you for an inheritance, you shall save alive nothing that breathes, but you shall utterly destroy them, the Hittites and the Amorites, the Canaanites and the Perizzites, the Hivites and the Jebusites, as the Lord your God has commanded: that they may not teach you to do according to all their abominable practices which they have done in the service of their gods, and so to sin against the Lord your God. [20.16]

These injunctions are clearly *post eventum* reconstructions of what ought to have happened much earlier on, because the historical and archaeological evidence is that in fact the occupation of the so-called Promised Land was not achieved over a short number of years by a single invading force of Israelites.

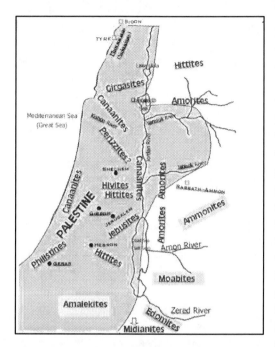

Rather, the population was a mixture of newcomers from Egypt, nomadic groups from elsewhere who settled in the hill country, migrants from local cities who joined them, established clans who were not uprooted from their existing villages, and so on. Existing religious practices continued alongside the worship of Yahweh for many centuries, until in the 7th century BC there were strenuous efforts to uproot them, whose guiding charter was formulated in the book of Deuteronomy. Its commendation of wholesale slaughter might seem to be much at odds with the earlier principle of 'proportionate response', until one realises that a Yahwistic mindset could not have conceived anything more evil than the rejection of God in favour of his rivals, false gods who led whole peoples astray. The near-contemporary prophecies of Ezekiel make it clear that God's wrath is certainly not confined to non-Jews: mass extermination of the faithless in Jerusalem itself is also required, though the inclusion of 'little children' as targets seems totally barbaric:

The shaded zone indicates the land 'coveted' (or 'claimed') by the Israelites. Before Joshua's campaign began a number of other tribes occu¬pied this territory. The map gives some idea of their location.

> Pass through the city ... and smite ... show no pity; slay old men outright, young men and maidens, little children and women. [Ezek 9.5-6]

It is, however, important to note that this fanatical streak is by no means entirely representative of the Old Testament ethos. Despite examples of sheer ruthless cruelty such as David's cold-blooded slaughter of Moabite captives [2 Sam 8.2] and Amaziah's troops throwing 'ten thousand men of Seir' off a cliff top to be dashed to pieces [2 Chron 25.12], there are other passages which attempt to limit the extent of devastation. For example, fighting between Judah and their 'brethren' in Israel is not to be pursued too relentlessly [1 Sam 2.27], even when their king is perceived to be an idolater [1 Kgs 12.21ff]. Subsequently Elisha insists that Aramaean prisoners should be well-treated and allowed to return home [2 Kgs 6.22-23 cf. David's assistance to the lone Egyptian who has been fighting for the Amalekites in 1 Sam 30.11]. In his day Amos castigated neighbouring tribes for failing to respect 'the covenant of brotherhood', for carrying 'into exile a whole people', for casting off 'all pity', for ripping up 'women with child'.

Nevertheless, there was no intention to propagate Israel's religion by imposing it elsewhere. It had no interest in making converts outside its own territory; although, if – duly impressed by the blessings bestowed by Israel's God – they came flocking to worship him in Jerusalem, that would itself be a further blessing. The rationale for holy war was quite simple. Over the centuries the land had suffered many setbacks and invasions: 'These we now see were God's way of punishing us for our lack of loyalty to him. The way forward is for us to keep the covenant he made with us and for our land to be cleansed of any disloyalty, by force if necessary. If only they had so kept the faith in time past!'

Yet not long after the Deuteronomists had codified their thinking, disaster struck again. The Babylonians invaded, and from then on the people of Israel were never in a position to fight their own battles. Not until the guerilla troops of the Maccabaeans in the 2nd century BC rose up in protest against their Greek overlords' desecration of the Temple was there any significant heeding of the Deuteronomic call to arms.

Meanwhile, new ideas had emerged in terms of one's personal response to provocation. The book of Proverbs records some of this wisdom:

> If your enemy is hungry, give him bread to eat; and if he is thirsty, give him water to drink; for you will heap   coals of fire on his head, and the Lord will reward you. [25.21-22]

38

Occasionally it includes advice for dealing with those who wield power:

> With patience a ruler may be persuaded, and a soft tongue will break a bone. [25.15]

> A wise man scales the city of the mighty and brings down the stronghold in which they trust. [21.22]

> The beginning of strife is like letting out water; so quit before the quarrel breaks out. [17.14]

It would seem that by now diplomacy is generally to be preferred to outright war, although the thinking is not without a degree of naivety:

> The righteous will never be removed, but the wicked will not dwell in the land. [10.30]

As we now know, the subsequent history of 'the land' shows how much in vain was this hope. For most of the two millennia that followed, Jews lived in the Diaspora in uneasy tension with Gentiles. Sometimes, as in medieval Spain for many centuries, there was mutual acceptance of different cultures and traditions; but at other times Jews retreated into ghettos and faced degrees of ostracism and persecution. The biblical vision of a promised land where only true religion would be found proved to be a mirage. As some Jews today recognise, one of the fundamental lessons that all human beings have to learn is the art of living with others who are different from oneself. In a radio programme last year, a Polish Jew put it like this: 'If you cannot live with the Other, you cannot live in this world.'

Indeed, the biblical concept of a land reserved by God exclusively for a particular people has always been nonsensical, given that from the dawn of mankind there has been a ceaseless movement of tribes and indivi-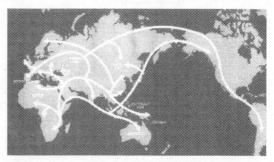duals across the globe, potentially bringing enrichment both to themselves and to those with whom they newly mingle. Nor were the biblical compilers unaware of this phenomenon:

> These are the families of the sons of Noah, according to their genealogies, in their nations; and from these the nations spread abroad after the flood. [Gen 10.32]

Yet here, as one scholar has expressed it: 'Alternative perspectives are juxtaposed in such a way as to undermine the dominant ideology' – by which he means Israelite separatism. He cites, for example, Genesis 9.27 which 'presents an eirenic picture of the descendants of Japheth living in the tents of Shem ... the two lineages are happily engaged in social intercourse.' Ham's descendants are viewed less favourably, and the following chapter 10 demonstrates why: they are empire builders (or in Jerome's word 'tyrants'), and Babel is among their possessions. Chapter 11 tells us what happened there – the erection of its tower was seen as an assertion of human autonomy and so was a direct challenge to God. Josephus, a 1st century Jew, described this as 'audacious', 'insolent', and 'contemptuous'. He commented on the tower's height: 'Lest God seek once again to flood the earth, this tower would be higher than the water, and thus his former destruction would be avenged.' The biblical text continues by describing God's reaction:

> The Lord said, 'Behold, they are one people, and they have all one language; and this is only the beginning of what they will do; and nothing that they propose to do will now be impossible for them ...
> So the Lord scattered them abroad over the face of all the earth.
> [Gen 11.6, 8]

So, whatever Israel's own future might be, there are distinct warnings here against any states that become over-bearing and too self-contained for their own good. Defensive walls should perhaps never be too impregnable.

Indeed, alternative perspectives about the Promised Land can also be found within the Hebrew scriptures. Its status is less certain in some of the later writings:

> I am thy passing guest, a sojourner, like all my fathers. [Ps 39.12]

> The land shall not be sold in perpetuity, for the land is mine; for you are strangers and sojourners with me. [Lev 25.23]

> We are sojourners, as all our fathers were ... and there is no abiding. [1 Chron 29.15]

It is worth noting how the Torah itself, in concluding with the death of Moses, God's prophet *par excellence*; records that he is buried in an unmarked grave well outside the territory being sought by Israel [Deut 34.6]: arguably therefore the final editors accepted that absolute possession of their own land was likewise an unattainable goal for Israel. They must be content, as the descendants of Shem [Gen 11.10-32], to coexist with others. There are also verses in Leviticus which serve to remind Israelites of God's makeshift provision for them:

> You shall dwell in booths for seven days; all that are native in Israel shall dwell in booths, that your generations may know that I made the people of Israel dwell in booths when I brought them out of the land of Egypt. [Lev 23.42-43]

This instruction is still heeded by observant Jews. So Miriam Lipis writes in the compendium *Jewish Topographies: Visions of Space, Traditions of Place*:

> A *succah* is a thatched booth with at least three walls, and must be built anew every year.

Alongside this regular reminder of the transitory nature of human existence and the impermanence of any established base, it is salutary to read the counter-narrative of how Abram (*sic*) and Lot parted:

> And Lot lifted up his eyes, and saw that the Jordan valley was well watered everywhere like the garden of the Lord, like the land of

41

> Egypt, in the direction of Zo'ar; this was before the Lord destroyed
> Sodom and Gomor'rah. [Gen 13.10]

So the Bible (in its reference here to Sodom) insists that the fulfilment of God's 'promise' depends even more upon human qualities than those of the land. Further, the insecurity of an individual's life may sometimes be writ large in the life of a nation, especially if collectively it fails to live up to its calling – hence Job's response to his own deprivations should be kept in mind:

> Naked I came from my mother's womb, and naked shall I return; the
> Lord gave, and the Lord has taken away; blessed be the name of the
> Lord. [Job 1.21]

Since many wars are fought over disputed tracts of land and there can be few nations that at some point in their history have not sought to expand their territorial claims by force, it is important to consider somewhat further the paradigmatic Jewish claim to their own inalienable land. In the aftermath of the Holocaust (or *Shoah*, meaning 'destruction' in Hebrew) might not any alternative reading of the Abrahamic covenant appear insensitive, if not open to the accusation of anti-Semitism? Edward Kessler has pointed out that Jews themselves are much divided on the issue. While for some 'traditional biblical interpretation provides the means to come to terms with the Shoah', for others 'the Jewish Bible ... must be struggled with, if necessary fought against'. He concludes:

> The majority of Jews are intensely aware ... of the inherent danger in the use of the fulfilment of biblical prophecy as the sole basis for Jewish attachment to the Land of Israel.

The Zionist movement itself began in earnest in the late 19th century. Its most significant boost was the Balfour Declaration of 1917.

Foreign Office,
November 2nd, 1917.

Dear Lord Rothschild,

I have much pleasure in conveying to you, on behalf of His Majesty's Government, the following declaration of sympathy with Jewish Zionist aspirations which has been submitted to, and approved by, the Cabinet

"His Majesty's Government view with favour the establishment in Palestine of a national home for the Jewish people, and will use their best endeavours to facilitate the achievement of this object, it being clearly understood that nothing shall be done which may prejudice the civil and religious rights of existing non-Jewish communities in Palestine, or the rights and political status enjoyed by Jews in any other country"

I should be grateful if you would bring this declaration to the knowledge of the Zionist Federation.

Jewish settlement in part of Kenya had in fact been proposed earlier (in 1903) in response to pogroms taking place in Russia, but Palestine rapidly became the preferred destination. Perhaps surprisingly, the Zionist headquarters at this time were in Berlin, backed by the Kaiser. Surprisingly too, when the Balfour Declaration was first drafted it was resisted by the only Jewish member of the cabinet, Edwin Samuel Montagu, who was opposed to Zionism. As a result of his criticisms the text was modified, with the addition of the clauses protecting non-Jews in Palestine and the rights of Jews elsewhere. What is less obvious was the growing split in the Zionist movement itself between Orthodox Jewry, whose thinking reflected biblical ideas, and secular Jews who were essentially nationalists.

When eventually after WW2 the United Nations voted to partition the Holy Land and to make provision for a Jewish state, this might seem to have at last fulfilled the Deuteronomic vision. Yet the future scale of

43

Jewish immigration with an increasingly secular dimension may be considered to have betrayed that vision, while of course the treatment of non-Jews both within Israel's borders and without has signally failed to offer the protection that Montagu saw as vital. He predicted that a Jewish state would increase anti-Semitism worldwide, and he was probably right. There is surely little difference between a country that upholds Jewish ethnicity and one that is purely 'Aryan' (as in Nazi Germany) – both are liable to promote intolerance and injustice. The same holds for their religious counterparts, and for the very concept of a 'state' religion which can seldom allow for the *development* of religious truth.

The warnings are there for Britain too, which is in some danger at the present time of succumbing to anti-immigration fever. Such xenophobia may be likened to king Canute trying to stop the waves flooding ashore! Or, to revert to the Bible, Deuteronomic teaching, while an understandable reaction to severe threats of foreign invasion, was in effect a nationalistic ideology based on a limited perception of God's universal sovereignty.

Sadly, such teaching was not absorbed only by Jews, but by others who were influenced by them. I refer here in the first place to Muhammad and his revelations in the early 7th century AD. As noted in previous Lent lectures (now published by Mzuni Press under the title *Emerging Scriptures*), the Qur'an is deeply in debt to biblical narratives and ideas, even though the version in which Muhammad received them had been filtered through a long process of oral transmission which included apocryphal additions and rabbinic revisions. His main concern was the maintenance of monotheistic belief, which – as in Deuteronomy – implied the destruction of all idols and conceivably of idol worshippers. How (and where) this goal was to be achieved is not entirely clear, since different verses of the Qur'an imply weaker or stronger measures according to the way Muslim fortunes developed in Muhammad's own lifetime. As not infrequently with the qur'anic text, the key issue of earlier verses being abrogated by later ones has never been fully resolved – even when there is a reasonable degree of chronological certainty. This therefore (as with the Bible) leaves it open for different factions to give prominence to their preferred interpretations, a point noted by early Muslim exegetes as well as modern scholars.

A word first though about the term *jihad*, which means 'striving' – yet always *fi sabil Allah*, 'in the path of God'. Its most important sense is the inner striving necessary for every individual believer, but the outward manifestation includes a range of peaceful initiatives, such as 'striving with the tongue', striving through education', striving by propagating the faith', quite apart from the use of force. Some form of holy war is certainly not the only way forward, nor is it necessarily the most effective way of achieving the desired end. As the biblical writers came to appreciate, much depends upon circumstances – and the need to consider the longer term consequences of any actions.

Thus, in what is generally agreed to be the earliest period of Muhammad's revelations (his time at Mecca) when he had relatively few supporters but much local opposition, he was warned to avoid conflict:

> Proclaim openly what you have been commanded [to say], and ignore the idolaters. We are enough for you against all those who ridicule your message. [Q 15.94-95]

Further happenings on the ground seemed to alert Muhammad for the need to respond occasionally with some force:

> Call [people] to the way of the Lord with wisdom and good teaching. Argue with them in the most courteous way, for your Lord knows best who has strayed from his way and who is rightly guided. If you [believers] have to respond to an attack, make your response proportionate, but it is best to stand fast. [Q 16.125-6]

The need for self-defence evidently began to loom larger as hostility against the Prophet increased:

> Those who have been attacked are permitted to take up arms because they have been wronged – God has the power to help them – those who have been driven from their homes only for saying, 'Our Lord is God'. If God did not repel some people by means of others, many monasteries, churches, synagogues, and mosques, where God's name is much invoked, would have been destroyed. God is sure to help those who help his cause – God is strong and mighty. [Q 22.39-40]

45

A particularly interesting feature of these verses is the apparent readiness to defend not only Muslims, but also Christians and Jews, who are also 'People of the Book' sharing Muhammad's Abrahamic faith – his monotheism. But once again this holy war must observe important limitations:

> Fight in God's cause against those who fight you, but do not overstep the limits: God does not love those who overstep the limits. Kill them wherever you encounter them, and drive them out from where they drove you out, for persecution is more serious than killing [*i.e. killing them within the precincts of the Sacred Mosque*]. If they do fight you, kill them – this is what disbelievers deserve – but if they stop, then God is most forgiving and merciful. Fight them until there is no more persecution, and worship is devoted to God. If they cease hostilities, there can be no [further] hostility, except towards aggressors. [Q 2. 190-3]

This passage reiterates the concept of war as essentially for the purposes of self-defence, and is thought to date from the phase that followed the *hijra* (the 'migration') of 622 AD when Muhammad was invited north to the town then known as Yathrib, but afterwards as Medina, where he established a strong base with his followers. The recurrent problem there was the frequency of attacks by the Meccan tribesmen on Muslim caravan trains, which brought a new dimension to the hostilities. It seems that Muhammad's policy changed in order to pre-empt attacks and ambushes i.e. his followers were allowed to take the initiative in seeking out those they termed 'the idolaters' with the intent of destroying them before they could do any harm. *Sura* 9.1-2, however, refers to a treaty made at the Sacred Mosque in which Muhammad subsequently undertook to let the idolaters move freely about for four months of each year. The *sura* continues:

> When the forbidden months are over, wherever you encounter the idolaters, kill them, seize them, besiege them, wait for them at every lookout post; but if they repent, maintain the prayer, and pay the prescribed alms, let them go on their way, for God is most forgiving and merciful. If any one of the idolaters should seek your protection, grant it to him so that he may hear the word of God. [Q 9.5-6]

Counted among the idolaters by now were those Christians and Jews whose faith was defective:

46

> Fight those of the People of the Book who do not [truly] believe in God and the Last Day, who do not forbid what God and his Messenger have forbidden, who do not obey the rule of justice, until they pay the tax promptly and agree to submit. [Q 9.29]

Evidently some of Muhammad's followers were reluctant to be called to such repeated hostilities:

> Fighting has been ordained for you, though it is hard for you. You may dislike something although it is good for you, or like something although it is bad for you: God knows and you do not. [Q 2.216]

This brandishing of divine instructions inaccessible to any but the Prophet himself may perhaps evoke recent claims by Western leaders to know better than anyone else what is for their country's good. Whereas Muhammad can elsewhere urge his audience to 'use their reason', here he asks them to trust solely to the revelation that he alone has received – and if some hesitate he can berate them:

> Those who turn on their heels after being shown guidance are duped and tempted by Satan; they say to those who hate what God has sent down, 'We will obey you in some matters'. [Q 47.25-26]

Indeed, in this *sura* 47 he can suggest that such people are 'corrupt at heart':

> If you turn away now, could it be that you will go on to spread corruption all over the land and break your ties of kinship? [Q 47.22]

Thus, he posits that any refusal to respond to the Prophet's call to arms is (1) satanically inspired (2) liable to corrupt Islamic faith on a much broader scale and (3) a denial of their tribal loyalties. No room for conscientious objection here – blind obedience is demanded.

In the Qur'an, therefore, there appears to be a shift from the avoidance of conflict to the necessity of self-defence, but then to the greater challenge of eliminating idolatry altogether. Unlike the Deuteronomic teachings, purity of faith is not intended just for a Holy Land, but for the entire planet – clearly an objective learnt from Christians rather than from Jews.

The assumption seems to be that so long as any so-called 'disbelief' is allowed to remain, the believers will face persecution:

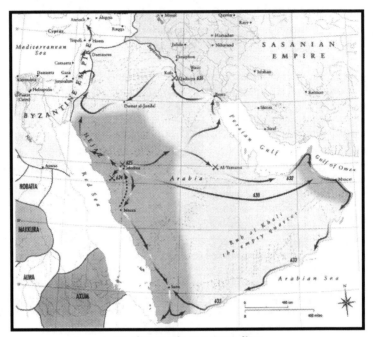

**Muslim territory expanding
at the time of Muhammad's death in 632**

[Believers], fight them until there is no more persecution, and all worship is devoted to God alone. [Q 8.39]

The prospect of a world where freedom of religion is the norm, in which Islam would be tolerated, was no doubt inconceivable to Muhammad, given the circumstances of his own day and age. But it is surely arguable that, just as qur'anic revelation once developed in response to the contemporary situation, so today its interpretation needs to relate to a very different context. Sadly, not all Muslims see it this way and take their cue from the last quoted verse, their aim being to wage a global campaign to eliminate what they see as unbelief wherever it occurs – in particular, to target Christians and Jews despite the fact already noted that both groups are more often than not regarded by the Qur'an as

48

fellow believers, being Peoples of the Book. Hence, neither faith community is, according to at least some of its teachings, a fitting target for Muslim hostility against idolatry:

> The believers, the Jews, the Christians, and the Sabians – all those who believe in God and the Last Day and do   good – will have their rewards with the Lord. [Q 2.62]

> Any who direct themselves wholly to God and do good will have their reward with their Lord. [Q 2.112]

However, in hastening the longed-for day when 'all worship is devoted to God alone' the discovery that few Jews and Christians were prepared to align themselves completely with the faith of the true believers may even in Muhammad's lifetime have suggested that more was at stake than tolerance for qur'anic teachings. Initially he conceived his role as God's Messenger as directed to Arab speakers:

> We have sent down the Qur'an to give judgement in the Arabic language. [Q 13.37]

> We have never sent a messenger who did not use his own people's language to make things clear for them. [Q 14.4]

> The scripture of Moses was revealed before it as a guide and a mercy, and this is a scripture confirming it in the Arabic language to warn those who do evil and bring good news for those who do good. [Q 46.12]

> The trustworthy Spirit brought it down to your heart, so that you could bring warning in a clear Arabic tongue. [Q 26.193-4 cf. 43.3]

Muhammad evidently perceived Christianity (which 'confirms the Torah') as a later variant of Judaism and seems to have understood his core message as a distillation of what both these faiths taught:

> Say, 'I am nothing new among God's messengers. I do not know what will be done with me or you; I only follow what is revealed to me; I only warn plainly.' [Q 46.9]

Nevertheless he seems to have begun to see his role much more distinctively. With the Hour of God's judgement drawing closer he could also believe himself to be God's final and definitive messenger – the 'seal of the prophets' [Q 33.40]. If so, two implications perhaps follow:

49

- Previous 'scriptures' may be subject to amendment:

  There was a Scripture for every age: God erases or confirms wherever He will, and the source of Scripture is with Him. [Q 13.39]

- Muhammad's message was not limited to those of Arab tongue:

  This is a message to all people, so that they may be warned by it. [Q 14.52]

  Say, 'People, I am the Messenger of God to you all, from Him who has control over the heavens and the earth.' [Q 7.158]

This would imply that tolerance – mere coexistence – was insufficient; submission (the meaning of the word *Islam*) must be required, and in the eyes of some Muslims this could justify the waging of Holy War to subdue any whose beliefs and practices failed to cohere entirely with their own.

It does not at all follow that the early conquests and the rapid expansion of Arab control necessarily had religious subjugation as a prime motivation. The fighting that escalated after Muhammad's death was generally neither a Just War nor a Holy War, but a land grab that took advantage of regional weaknesses especially within the Byzantine and Persian spheres of influence. The appeal to the many Arab tribesmen who participated (some of whom had previously been engaged as mercenaries in the imperial armies) was surely too the booty that they obtained. They were perhaps not unduly mindful of the Qur'an's teaching that the more important 'rewards' or 'gains' promised to believers are those of Paradise:

  You desire the transient goods of this world, but God desires the Hereafter [for you]. [Q 8.67]

There are certainly modern parallels, but the ruthlessness of both Isis and Boko Haram (in north-eastern Nigeria) far exceeds any brutality witnessed in the initial Muslim campaigns. Today's 'extremists' appear to have little in common with their co-religionists beyond their brandishing of Allah's name. Indeed, in the case of Boko Haram its very title – which means 'books are forbidden' – points to widespread illiteracy that embraces the religious sphere. The movement is in reality familiar tribal aggression masquerading under false pretensions. Its leader, self-styled

50

'Emir' Abu Bakr Shekau, has his headquarters in Gwoza near the frontier with Cameroon. The surrounding area is the homeland of Shekau's own ethnic group, the Kanuri. From this base Shekau's fighters strike across a vast area, both to gain territory and to enslave women and children who are then forced to renounce any faith but (his version of) Islam.

This contemptuous disregard for Christianity and the denial of religious freedom is quite at odds with the Arab conquests in the century following Muhammad's death. There was certainly no attempt initially to impose a new state religion – this only began to take shape under 'Abd al-Malik who was Caliph from 685-705. Even then both Christians and Jews were usually allowed to continue practising their own faiths, and

Abu Bakr Shekau speaking in the name of Allah 'the Merciful'

sometimes received help in building or restoring their places of worship. Without their active involvement in the administrative affairs of the new regime, it would have been hard for the Arab infrastructure to function effectively; and in any case if they all converted to Islam, where – instead of the taxes imposed upon them – would the much needed funds be derived to run public finances? Thus, in those early days it would certainly appear that Muslims usually heeded the qur'anic note of caution:

> You who believe, be careful when you go to fight in God's way, and
> do not say to someone who offers you a greeting of peace, 'You are
> not a believer'. [Q 4.94]

The aim was not to create mayhem but to win control, and peaceful means i.e. treaties were much to be preferred over the cruder methods of slaughter. Yet there were certain obvious occasions when the injunction 'to fight in God's way' was ignored. Not one but two civil wars (656-661 and 683-692) broke out in the 7th century between different Muslim factions, each wishing to grasp power. The 'enemy' was not unbelief, but believers from other Arab tribes!

The more detailed teachings of the Qur'an only gradually became more widely known from the later 7th century onwards. Different attempts to record 'the recitation' started to appear in written form, but it was later still when Muslim missionaries as such appeared on the scene to impart its truths to unbelievers. It will also be clear that the sometimes conflicting teachings of the Qur'an required careful reflection, and as new situations were encountered Muslims often relied upon Muhammad's own example as well as the recorded *suras* to inform their behaviour. As with the earlier Abrahamic faiths, a corpus of elucidation emerged, much of it in the compilations known as the *hadith*. It is here that we find attention being given not only as to when war should be undertaken but the limitations on how it should be fought. Thus, the *hadith* specifies, 'Do not kill women, children, or the elderly, nor cut down trees, burn buildings, or kill cattle or sheep except for eating purposes.' Or again, 'Do not burn palm trees and do not flood vegetation. Do not pillage or betray'. Such details may be paralleled in the development of just war theory from the Christian perspective, which is considered in the next chapter.

A final word may be in order here about the wider scene. It is not only the Abrahamic faiths stemming from the Hebrew tradition that have examined the ethics of war: the same is found in the major religions of Asia – Hinduism, Buddhism and Sikhism, for example – where a similar range of issues occurs. Thus, in the *Bhagavad Gita* the god Krishna reminds Arjuna that to fight for peace, justice and truth is to fulfil the law of God. The *Rig Veda* warns, however, that the warrior should not poison the tip of his arrow, nor should he attack the sick or the old, a child, or a woman or from behind: all these are sinful and lead to hell even if the warrior wins the battle.

Nanak (the first Sikh guru) wrote, 'No one is my enemy, no one is a foreigner; with all I am at peace. God within us renders us incapable of hate and prejudice.' Yet Sikhism became more militant from the time of Arjan, a later guru who was martyred; his successor taught that military action was sometimes necessary to promote justice and protect the innocent, and the tradition grew up of fighting all oppression.

In other words, the march of time and the events of history have usually resulted in changing attitudes to war. We shall find the same is true in Christian teaching.

Indra, god of war in the Rig Veda

3. Christian Thinking about War

The writings of the New Testament almost all date from the 1st century AD when the Church was in its infancy. Their collective testimony focuses on the life, death and resurrection of Jesus, including their impact on his disciples and on others who encountered him. There are few sayings of his which bear directly upon the issue of war, although his personal renunciation of retaliation against his accusers has obviously been hugely influential. In the following centuries it was his readiness to die for others that inspired the Christian martyrs and informed the generally pacifist teachings of early church fathers such as Tertullian and Origen.

However, when the emperor Constantine was himself converted at the beginning of the 4th century, the situation changed dramatically. Not only did Christians become considerably more numerous, but – more to the point – many of those who held public responsibilities were converted too. Until now, most Christians had not had to face the question of how to respond to large scale aggression, for example, from invading tribes beyond the frontiers of the empire; their immediate concerns had been more locally confined to the seizure of their property or threats against their persons. Hence the development observed in the previous chapter within the Muslim community, whereby earlier *suras* dating from the days of Meccan persecution were possibly abrogated by those more relevant to their much stronger situation in Medina, was in fact very similar to the way Christians too modified their thinking according to circumstances. We noted something of the same happening in the Old Testament: as Jewish fortunes declined in the centuries of their subjection to neighbouring powers, so wisdom literature began to emphasise the virtues of diplomacy in place of conflict.

So attitudes towards war do change over the years, depending on the context. To give a more recent example: when German troops marched into Belgium in 1914, the response was a *declaration of war* that many Christian leaders in Britain endorsed. In 2014, however, when Russia annexed Crimea no one seems to have supported the sending of Western troops to reclaim the territory; the way forward was considered to be the imposition of *economic sanctions*, an option not apparently considered 100 years previously. (In fact, Edward Grey, who was then the Foreign Secretary, informed parliament that, unless Germany was halted by military means, there would be serious economic consequences for Britain. Whatever they might have been, it is unlikely that they would have proved nearly as dire as the effect of four long years of war.)

More recently still, Pope Francis remarked over the incursion of Islamic State jihadis into Northern Iraq:

> Where there is an unjust aggression, I can only say that it is legitimate to *stop* the unjust aggressor. I underscore the verb *to stop*. I am not saying *bomb* or *make war*, but *stop* him. The means by which he can be stopped must be evaluated. One single nation cannot judge how he is to be stopped. The United Nations is the proper forum to consider whether there has been unjust aggression and how to stop it.

His counsel is the fruit of many centuries of debate, which for Christians goes back to the time of Christ, whose most revered comment on the subject (to judge by its prominence in the Beatitudes) was 'Blessed are the peacemakers'. In Matthew's collection of Jesus' sayings known as the Sermon on the Mount, he expands his teaching by classifying 'anger' – the desire for vengeance – with 'killing', and urges his hearers to love their enemies and to pray for their persecutors:

> I say to you, Do not resist one who is evil. But if any one strikes you on the right cheek, turn to him the other also. [Mt 5.39]

In the same spirit he rebukes one of his disciples who is too ready to defend him against his arrest:

> One of those who were with Jesus stretched out his hand and drew his sword, and struck the slave of the high priest, and cut off his ear. Then Jesus said to him, "Put your sword back into its place; for all who take the sword will perish by the sword. [Mt 26.51-2]

Military personnel do feature in the New Testament, but to a limited extent. In Luke's Gospel, John the Baptist urges them to 'rob no one by violence or false accusation' and to 'be content with their wages'. Jesus praises a centurion for his faith, and it is a centurion standing by the cross who makes the confession 'Truly this man was the Son of God'. He is presumably one of the squad of soldiers who not long before has mocked and abused Jesus, but whose manner of dying has now paradoxically provoked a sea change in the centurion's heart and mind. Subsequently it is Matthew again who reports on the ineffectiveness of the guards put outside Jesus' tomb; they are powerless to prevent the Lord rising from the dead and emerging victorious from his grave. In the Fourth Gospel the actual moment of triumph is when Jesus is 'lifted up' on the Cross, drawing all men to him. Thus, the gospels display how the strong are in fact weak, and the weak made strong by God's help.

The point can be further illustrated by juxtaposing two further gospel verses. On one occasion Jesus is challenging the crowd to consider the cost of their discipleship:

> What king, going to encounter another king in war, will not sit down first and take counsel whether he is able with ten thousand to meet him who comes against him with twenty thousand? [Lk 14.31]

In worldly terms anyone entering upon a new enterprise would assess whether he can carry it through to a fitting conclusion – and a seriously outnumbered king would be very unlikely to engage an enemy in battle. Yet Jesus himself, although heavily outnumbered, is striving in God's cause and triumphs against the odds. So Caiaphas' cynical comment ironically proved much truer than he could ever have conceived

> It was Caiaphas who had given counsel to the Jews that it was expedient that one man should die for the people. [Jn 18.14]

Here we may recall that in many cultures both ancient and modern there are references to battles being settled by champions who represent their respective sides in single combat, which is certainly much less wasteful of human life than a war which drags on endlessly. In the Old Testament the obvious example is of the lightly armed David who defeats the opposing giant Goliath. Most likely it is a fictional narrative designed to stress the spiritual superiority of one whose five smooth stones symbolise the five books of the Jewish Torah. There is such strength in God's word that one stone alone suffices to slay the Philistine. So too the early Christian perspective was that despite all human opposition their salvation was assured through the sacrifice of one man Jesus Christ.

Yet the Church was not necessarily on a collision course with the secular power. Jesus himself had said:

> Render to Caesar the things that are Caesar's, and to God the things that are God's. [Mk 12.17]

Subsequently, however, he did remind Caesar's representative Pontius Pilate whence his authority actually derived:

> You would have no power over me unless it had been given you from above. [Jn 19.11]

So the Christian community was fully aware that their loyalty to the state was qualified. Paul, evidently a Roman citizen, certainly urges the practice of prayer for those in authority:

> First of all, then, I urge that supplications, prayers, intercessions, and thanksgivings be made for all men, for kings and all who are in high positions, that we may lead a quiet and peaceable life, godly and respectful in every way. [1 Tim 2.1-2]

Elsewhere he insists that the Christian's allegiance ultimately lies beyond any human institution:

> Do not be conformed to this world but be transformed by the renewal of your mind, that you may prove what is the will of God, what is good and acceptable and perfect. [Rom 12.2]

This is the apostles' common testimony, articulated in the book of Acts before the Jewish authorities:

> But Peter and the apostles answered, 'We must obey God rather than men.' [5.29 cf. Peter and John's similar reply to earlier questioning 4.19]

Christians have therefore always retained the right to act according to their conscience. In the early Church this was tested above all by the demands of the state to observe certain customary rituals which implied the acknowledgement of pagan gods and even the recognition of the Roman emperor as having divine status. This was one reason why military service was discouraged, since unacceptable oaths and sacrifices would have been required. Hence too the Roman empire, once appreciated for its *Pax Romana*, an age of peace and stability which allowed the Christian message to spread freely across the Mediterranean world, became increasingly identified with Babylon, the source of corruption and evil. This is the perspective of the closing book of the New Testament, the Apocalypse of John. From the middle of the 1st century onwards, sporadic persecution against Christians fostered a sense of the illegitimacy of the power wielded by state authorities. The gospel accounts of Jesus' clash with officialdom suggest that the latter was not to be trusted. In Francis Bacon's words, '"What is truth?" said jesting Pilate, and would not stay for an answer.' Even the people themselves (as we noted earlier) are unreliable, at first acclaiming Jesus enthusiastically but then later clamouring for his death. Of course, a different crowd may have been coerced into displaying hostility.

Until about the closing years of the 2nd century the attitude of the church was consistently pacifist. No Christian would become a soldier after baptism at least up to the time of Marcus Aurelius. Subsequently signs of compromise can be seen (to meet the defensive needs of the Roman Empire), but the pacifist trend continued strongly at least as far as the 4th century. Many sources exhorting Christians to conform to God's higher demands can be cited.

Tatian, one of the early Apologists, writes of his readiness to die to the world, 'repudiating the madness that is in it'. Aristides expressed the Christian counter-cultural approach as follows:

> Whatever Christians would not wish others to do to them, they do not to others. And they comfort their oppressors and make them their friends; they do good to their enemies. [Apol 15]

Subsequently we find Hippolytus of Rome being quite emphatic about military service. He insisted that 'If a believer seeks to become a soldier, he must be rejected, for he has despised God.' And Tertullian elaborates this ruling:

> How will a Christian man war, nay, how will he serve even in peace, without a sword, which the Lord has taken away? [On Idolatry 19]

Origen too observes that Christians would not, although able, wage war even if they had received authority to do so. He adds that the weapon of prayer is more powerful than the sword:

> As we by our prayers vanquish all demons who stir up war ... we in this way are much more helpful to the kings than those who go into the field to fight for them ... None fight better for the king than we do. We do not indeed fight under him, although he require it; but we fight on his behalf, forming a special army − an army of piety − by offering our prayers to God. [Contra Celsum 8.73]

Yet, despite such a firm ethos rejecting the use of violence and observing the inconsistency between 'what is called a crime when committed by an individual but a virtue when performed wholesale' (in the words of Cyprian of Carthage), it is clear that some Christians did perform military service in these earlier times, which is probably why much was written against the practice.

In the 4th century there was a significant change in the Church's approach, when the responsibility for maintaining peace and order devolved upon governors and officials who may well have belonged to the Church. There was at the very least a distinction to be drawn between following the path of non-resistance for oneself and intervening on behalf of others, especially those who were weak and helpless themselves.

Among the pioneering thinkers was Ambrose of Milan, who before his ordination had been governor of Liguria-Emilia and as such had been able to call upon the militia to resist hostile action and public violence. One of his principal writings was *De Officiis*, which spelt out the duties laid upon the Christian community and her leaders, not least in caring for others. Sometimes, he taught, we are called upon to defend others, and not so doing might well be a failure of neighbourly love. Yet much depended on the way we carry out such a responsibility: Ambrose's preferred option was 'not to look to arms but to the forces of peace.' He did nonetheless express the view in *De Fide* that an expedition against the Arian Goths might be the means not only of defending the Empire but of bringing them back into the orthodox fold. In *De Tobia* he argued that while war (and for that matter usury) against fellow believers or fellow Roman citizens was to be eschewed, against others it might be permitted. How it was to be waged was another matter altogether: here Ambrose in *De Officiis* drew upon ideas expressed two centuries earlier by the Roman writer and orator Cicero, who had argued that war is a defensive resort whose object is to promote peace, that it should spare non-combatants and be merciful to any who surrender, that only soldiers under oath of service could legitimately fight, and that the humanity of one's enemy must be recognised. He insisted that any agreements made should be honoured and no unfair advantage be taken of the enemy. Within those limitations he went so far as to praise anyone who defends his country at personal risk to himself.

The logic of his position led him to confess that force might also be used in the private sphere when others needed protection; so Moses' killing of the Egyptian who was beating a Hebrew slave [Exod 2.11-12] was not merely to be condoned but actually to be praised as an act of virtue. This did not mean that force used in the defence of one's own person was at all justified, and when imperial troops threatened his basilica in Milan he was equally emphatic in being quiescent. Resistance to personal threats amounted in his view to destroying one's trust in God and one's inner spiritual calling. True motivation must always be a preference for a divine ordering of life above one's limited human instincts. Yet, if Ambrose certainly made advances upon the pacifist emphases of previous centuries, at this point he left unresolved the issue of marrying the necessary external use of restraint with the internal disposition of love. In the first chapter I described how this very tension was the underlying factor in so-called 'shell-shock'.

Augustine of Hippo was very much influenced by Ambrose, whom he heard preach in Milan during the three years he spent there. Suitably 'formed and instructed' by scripture he and his son were baptised by Ambrose on Easter Eve 387. He had previously been a Manichean, and one of his polemical writings *Contra Faustum* was directed against Manichaeism around the year 400. The Manicheans regarded the God of the Old Testament as inferior to the perfectly good Father of Jesus in the New Testament, and his instructions to Moses on waging war as contrary to divine teaching. Augustine, who develops Ambrose' teaching on the Just War, counters the Manichean position as too simplistic. He then includes a remarkable passage dealing with the 'real' evils of war which addresses the issues that also concerned Ambrose:

> The real evils in war are love of violence, revengeful cruelty, fierce and implacable enmity, wild resistance, the lust of power and such like.

Thus, while Moses (as the editors of the Pentateuch portrayed him) may not have perfectly grasped God's intentions, Augustine considered that he was justified in obeying the highest authority he knew rather than pursuing any grandiose objectives of his own. It was always important in his view that war should be properly sanctioned by those who exercised the appropriate responsibility, and tended to assume that others should be quiescent in their acceptance of such decisions. If Moses was in fact rooting out forms of idolatry or other evils, this accorded with his often punitive model of war. Augustine wrote in one of his letters:

> Wars should be waged by the good, in order to curb licentious passions.

Nevertheless, he qualified his reading of the Old Testament in *Ad Faustum* as follows:

> The patriarchs and prophets have a kingdom in this world to show that these kingdoms too are given and taken away by God: the apostles and martyrs had no kingdom here, to show the desirability of the kingdom of heaven.

So the earlier scriptures serve as a stage in God's progressive revelation of what is truly good. The kind of peace we aim to enjoy under the conditions of this life (as he expressed it in *The City of God*) is 'rather the solace of our misery than the positive enjoyment of felicity'. Hence to fight as a form of self-defence for the protection of one's own goods might well accord with human laws but, given that many such goods are not always ours to command and so ought not to be cherished at all, they count for far less than the spiritual goods – the virtues and attributes of the soul – which are of eternal worth. Augustine's account of war is therefore invariably coloured by his focus upon our ultimate destiny.

His ideas proved to be very influential subsequently, particularly in relation to the *Reconquista* of Moorish Spain and the Crusades launched by various Popes to retake the Holy Land from its Muslim occupation. From the 8th to the 10th centuries Europe looked mainly to defend its own northern and eastern frontiers and left Spanish kings largely unsupported in their efforts to regain control of central and then southern Spain. These, although justifiable as self-defence, were not regarded as specifically religious wars until after about 1063 when it appears that the then Pope Alexander II promised indulgences to those engaged in an expedition against the city of Barbastro, since described as 'a crusade before the crusades'. His intervention seems to have promoted a descent into barbarity. The Andalusian Muslim jurist Ibn 'Abd al-Barr was among the witnesses of the fall of Barbastro. He described the aftermath as follows:

> Imāms and pious men, vergers and muezzins...are dragged away by the infidels like animals for sacrifice, they are brought to the butcher, they prostrate themselves humbly in the mosques which are then burnt and reduced to ashes while the infidels laugh and insult us, and our religion wails and weeps.

It is not entirely clear, however, that such attacks were always perceived in religious terms. At other times the word 'infidels' was replaced by the ethnic description 'Franks', so that the mounting aggression against Islam was seen rather as European belligerence rather than a Christian-motivated campaign. In fact, Muslim potentates often spent more time on conflict with co-religionist rivals than with the infidel. In the years 1110-1115 we even see Muslim rulers allying with Frankish princes against fellow Muslims (and their Frankish allies!). A few decades later, the Syrian Muslim aristocrat, Usama Ibn Munqidh, fraternised with Knights Templar and other Franks in Jerusalem. Again, far from expressing appreciation of Saladin's recovery of Jerusalem in 1187, the Abbasid Caliph in Baghdad looked askance at much of his activity, while in 1190 the Almohad Caliph of Morocco refused a request to assist Saladin because his ambassador would not address him by his proper title. Thus today's jihadist in-fighting is scarcely a novelty!

Nevertheless, what set out to be a 'holy war' in the shape of successive Crusades certainly lowered the barriers of conduct as required by the high ideals of a 'just war'. The danger had already been seen in Augustine's writings: in theory holy war could be seen as an act of love, curbing 'licentious passions' and rooting out heresy (which was the predominant view of Islam for many centuries); yet all too easily it could induce 'a love of violence and revengeful cruelty'. Recognising this tendency, medieval canon law developed its own remedy: after any battle soldiers were required to do penance as a precaution against having sinned by allowing themselves to have been overcome by 'wrong intentions'. Thus, after the Battle of Hastings in 1066 William the Conqueror founded Battle Abbey as a fitting expression of sorrow for the sins incurred in fighting and killing. It was not so much a matter of the deaths or injuries inflicted, as the moral character of the one who wielded the sword: had he, or had he not, descended into barbarity in his own disposition?

When Pope Urban II launched the so-called First Crusade in a sermon at Clermont in 1095 he spoke too of the harmful impact of conflicts taking place in the West and emphasised his vision of a new Christian society in the East. In the following decades the papacy developed his thinking: the purpose of a crusade was to bring about the renewal of a Christian world, with unity restored between East and West. In particular, it encouraged a lay spirituality with the foundation of new military or quasi-monastic orders (such as the Knights Hospitallers dating from the late 11th century, here illustrated with their Grand Master). These forms of religious life

developed in the West and spread much further afield to Cyprus, Asia Minor, Lebanon and the Holy Land itself.

Their object was to assist those who fought – in what was considered to be a legitimate defence of the Christian faith – to do so without losing their own souls:

> What does it profit a man, to gain the whole world and forfeit his life? [Mk 8.36]

Despite such lofty ideals, the Crusades proved disastrous for the Christian cause. The obsession with the recovery of the Holy Land lasted for 200 years and ended in failure. (Between 1096 and 1291 there were seven major Crusades and numerous minor ones: see the map below.)

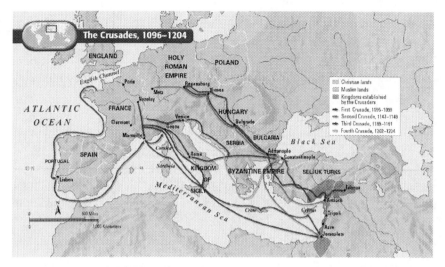

The First Crusade (1096-9) travelling *en route* through the Rhineland killed 8000 Jews in the first major European pogrom, and in capturing Jerusalem massacred its inhabitants. It established a Latin kingdom in Palestine which lasted until 1187. The Second Crusade (1147-9), preached by St Bernard, achieved little except the incidental seizure of Lisbon from the Moors by an English fleet. The Third Crusade (1189-92), which included Richard Cceur de Lion, failed to retake Jerusalem. The Fourth Crusade (1202-4) was diverted by the ambitions of the Doge of Venice to occupy Constantinople, slaughtering many of its inhabitants in the process. Three further efforts in the 13th century all ended up in Egypt or in Tunis, where St Louis of France himself died of the plague. When the last Christian stronghold in the Holy Land fell at Acre in 1291, there was no coherent response.

The conduct of the crusaders for much of the time was shocking, even to their contemporaries. They ravaged the countries through which they marched. The crusaders fought among themselves no less than against the infidel. Bernard, who had been recruited by Pope Eugenius III in 1145 to preach as an advocate for the crusading spirit, was far from being naive about it. He warned Louis VII of France of the consequences of unjust warfare, in which 'burnings are added to burnings and slaughter to slaughter'. In similar vein he wrote in his treatise *In Praise of the New Knighthood*:

What else moves you to wars and disputes except irrational flashes of anger, the thirst for empty glory, or the hankering after some earthly possession? It is surely not safe for reasons such as these.

As Augustine had done before him, he insisted that unjust warfare is not only injurious to the peace of the land; it threatens the well-being of the perpetrator before God. Motivation is therefore the key element, and the only motivation for crusading is to prevent Muslims from persecuting the Christian faithful should there prove to be no alternative way of restraining them. They should certainly not be killed simply because of their religion. Yet, he added, if the crusaders' hearts are not truly orientated towards God, it would be unsurprising if they suffer the same fate as those Israelites, who 'fell and perished because of their iniquity'.

Despite the undoubted acts of heroism by some crusaders which promoted the growth of medieval romances such as those featuring King Arthur and his knights (which gave Western militarism its unfounded Christian credentials), the Crusades had catastrophic consequences. After the sack of Constantinople the reunification of Christendom became virtually impossible, and after the repeated barbarism of the crusading armies against Muslim populations relations between Christianity and Islam were poisoned beyond any serious hope of repair. Western countries may have forgotten what happened all those centuries ago, supposedly in the name of Christ; but Muslims in the Middle East have not, and interventions in their region are readily seen as a continuation of that aggression. 'Arguably,' Norman Davies once wrote, 'the only fruit of the Crusades kept by the Christians was the apricot.'

Before the Crusades had finally petered out, St Thomas Aquinas, writing his *Summa Theologiae* in the late 1260s, gave a clear summary of how Christians in the later Middle Ages had come to understand the justification for the waging and conduct of war. In the previous century Gratian had codified canon law in his *Decretum*, where it was certainly envisaged that war against heretics could on occasion be justified. His commentators, the Decretists, argued that such war could be declared on the authority of the Pope, who indeed could also command Christians to fight. **Aquinas** derived much of his own magisterial thinking on the subject from Augustine, whom he quotes (often via Gratian) a number of times. The heart of his account [2.2.40] reads as follows:

In order for a war to be just, three things are necessary:

First, Augustine says: "The natural order conducive to peace among mortals demands that the power to declare and counsel war should be in the hands of those who hold the supreme authority."

Secondly, a just cause is required, namely that those who are attacked, should be attacked because they deserve it on account of some fault.

Thirdly, it is necessary that the belligerents should have a rightful intention, so that they intend the advancement of good, or the avoidance of evil. Hence Augustine says: "True religion looks upon as peaceful those wars that are waged not for motives of aggrandizement, or cruelty, but with the object of securing peace, of punishing evil-doers, and of uplifting the good."

These three necessary features certainly need much interpretation, to take account of particular – and indeed changing – circumstances. The way *authority* is exercised is today quite different from the situation in medieval Europe, when power was wielded by personal rulers and the concept of a 'state' had scarcely been formed. It was during the 16th century that the notion of sovereignty began to be developed by Jean Bodin in response to the French wars of religion. The idea of international law emerged around the same time, particularly in the writings of the Spanish theologians Francisco de Victoria and Francisco Suarez. Then an early milestone was reached in 1625 with Hugo Grotius' *De jure belli ac pacis* ('On the law of war and peace'). Essentially he presented a secularised version of Christian Just War theory, using rational arguments that would still hold even (in his memorable phrase) 'if God did not exist'. Three centuries later the first attempt to form a world 'authority' took shape as The League of Nations in the aftermath of WW1. It could not enforce decisions, but hoped to settle disputes by negotiation and arbitration. However, in the 1930s countries such as Germany and Italy withdrew from it.

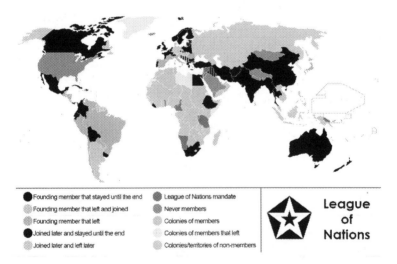

Founding member that stayed until the end
Founding member that left and joined
Founding member that left
Joined later and stayed until the end
Joined later and left later

League of Nations mandate
Never members
Colonies of members
Colonies of members that left
Colonies/territories of non-members

League of Nations

Following WW2 a renewed attempt was made in the form of the United Nations, which survives to this day. Chapter VII of its charter concerns the waging of war. Under article 51, there is 'the inherent right of individual or collective self-defence if an armed attack occurs against a Member of the United Nations, until the Security Council has taken measures necessary to maintain international peace and security'. Under article 39 pre-emptive action may be authorised: 'the Security Council shall determine the existence of any threat to the peace, breach of the peace, or act of aggression and shall make recommendations, or decide what measures shall be taken in accordance with Articles 41 and 42, to maintain or restore international peace and security'.

Yet as we know, sometimes governments fail to act to protect their people, and guerilla fighting or resistance movements develop in their stead; these may well be regarded as legitimate so long as there is a reasonable hope of success. Or again, since 2005 the United Nations has been steadily clarifying the principle known as R2P (Responsibility to Protect) which last year was enunciated in the form of three 'pillars': (1) each individual state has the primary responsibility to protect its populations from atrocities; (2) the international community must assist states in upholding these obligations; and (3) when a state is unable or unwilling to protect its civilians, the international community has a responsibility to take collective action in a timely and decisive manner.

As for **just cause** ('ius ad bellum') it is understood that war should normally be the last resort when all feasible forms of negotiation have failed; but even then, there must be sufficient proportion between the good that may be achieved and the harm incurred in the process – the likely cost of any victory must be taken into account, and its achievement must be realistically attainable. The means of waging war ('ius in bello') must also be kept within moral bounds; hence the targeting of civilians, the abuse of prisoners, disregard for the rights of neutral countries and so on, are inadmissible. Such issues are of course now generally covered by international agreements such as Geneva Conventions. Since nuclear war must inevitably afflict civilian life on a large scale, it would seem, according to Christian ideas, to be unjust in its very character: its long-term harmful consequences arguably outweigh any positive outcomes. Medieval prohibitions such as the banning of poisoned arrows and of environmental destruction have their modern equivalents (for example, the outlawing of biological or chemical weapons) which began to be considered over a hundred years ago in conferences held in the Hague or in Geneva.

Finally, regarding **rightful intention**, it is quite possible that while objective grounds for war exist, a nation may decide to fight for the wrong motives. This undoubtedly occurred to some extent at the time of the Crusades. The Christian tradition would uphold the rights of conscientious objectors in such circumstances; some might be convinced pacifists in any case (as we shall see in the final chapter), making legitimate appeal to the Church's early teachings, while others might have objections against a particular war only.

We may recall at this point Pope Benedict XV's firm opposition to the First World War. In July 1915 he described it as 'butchery which has been disgracing Europe for a whole year'. Whether or not there was just cause for such fighting – *jus ad bellum* – he was appalled by the extent of the slaughter, quite disproportionate to any justice that might be achieved. Thus for him it failed the test of *jus in bello*. It has to be said that he was supported by the Catholic bishops of Germany, who issued a statement explicitly admitting the churches' guilt in fostering a climate of warmongering. Alas, Catholic bishops in England contemptuously ignored the Pope's appeal.

Since then, there have been many more papal interventions appealing for peace, especially in the last fifty years. The most frequently quoted are words of Paul VI's impassioned plea to the UN in 1965: 'No more war! Never again war!' Two months later he promulgated the Pastoral Constitution on the Church in the Modern World (known as *Gaudium et Spes*) which arose from Vatican 2. This included two paragraphs 78 and 79, considering respectively peace and then war. Here are a few extracts:

> We cannot fail to praise those who renounce the use of violence in the vindication of their rights and who resort to methods of defence which are otherwise available to weaker parties too, provided this can be done without injury to the rights and duties of others or of the community itself.

> Even though recent wars have wrought physical and moral havoc on our world, the devastation of battle still goes on day by day in some part of the world. Indeed, now that every kind of weapon produced by modern science is used in war, the fierce character of warfare threatens to lead the combatants to a savagery far surpassing that of the past. Furthermore, the complexity of the modern world and the intricacy of international relations allow guerrilla warfare to be drawn out by new methods of deceit and subversion. In many causes the use of terrorism is regarded as a new way to wage war.

70

Contemplating this melancholy state of humanity, the council wishes, above all things else, to recall the permanent binding force of universal natural law and its all-embracing principles. Man's conscience itself gives ever more emphatic voice to these principles. Therefore, actions which deliberately conflict with these same principles, as well as orders commanding such actions are criminal, and blind obedience cannot excuse those who yield to them. The most infamous among these are actions designed for the methodical extermination of an entire people, nation or ethnic minority. Such actions must be vehemently condemned as horrendous crimes. The courage of those who fearlessly and openly resist those who issue such commands merits supreme commendation.

On the subject of war, quite a large number of nations have subscribed to international agreements aimed at making military activity and its consequences less inhuman. Their stipulations deal with such matters as the treatment of wounded soldiers and prisoners. Agreements of this sort must be honoured ... Moreover, it seems right that laws make humane provisions for the case of those who for reasons of conscience refuse to bear arms, provided however, that they agree to serve the human community in some other way.

Certainly, war has not been rooted out of human affairs. As long as the danger of war remains and there is no competent and sufficiently powerful authority at the international level, governments cannot be denied the right to legitimate defence once every means of peaceful settlement has been exhausted.

Those too who devote themselves to the military service of their country should regard themselves as the agents of security and freedom of peoples. As long as they fulfill this role properly, they are making a genuine contribution to the establishment of peace.

'War,' noted John Paul II, 'is not inevitable; it is always a defeat for humanity.' His successor Benedict XVI condemned (in his World Peace Day message of 2006) the false security placed in nuclear weapons: 'Such a point of view is not only baneful, it is completely fallacious'. And less than two years ago the present Pope Francis commented: 'Death is not answered with the language of death. In the silence of the Cross the uproar of weapons ceases and the language of reconciliation, forgiveness, dialogue and peace is spoken. Violence and war are never the way to peace.' War, as in Salvador Dali's foreboding *Premonitions of War* (1936), is a self-destructive monster.

Pope Francis words have a similar sense of urgency. Perhaps however the measured tones of the *Catechism of the Catholic Church* (1994) may offer a more comprehensive summary of recent church teaching.

Avoiding war

2308 As long as the danger of war persists and there is no international authority with the necessary competence and power, governments cannot be denied the right of lawful self-defence, once all peace efforts have failed.

2309 The strict conditions for legitimate defence by military force require rigorous consideration. The gravity of such a decision makes it subject to rigorous conditions of moral legitimacy. At one and the same time: - the damage inflicted by the aggressor on the nation or community of nations must be lasting, grave, and certain; - all other means of putting an end to it must have been shown to be impractical or ineffective; - there must be serious prospects of success; - the use of arms must not produce evils and disorders graver than the evil to be eliminated. The power of modem means of destruction weighs very heavily in evaluating this condition.

These are the traditional elements enumerated in what is called the "just war" doctrine. The evaluation of these conditions for moral legitimacy belongs to the prudential judgment of those who have responsibility for the common good.

2310 Public authorities, in this case, have the right and duty to impose on citizens the obligations necessary for national defence. Those who are sworn to serve their country in the armed forces are servants of the security and freedom of nations. If they carry out their duty honourably, they truly contribute to the common good of the nation and the maintenance of peace.

2311 Public authorities should make equitable provision for those who for reasons of conscience refuse to bear arms; these are nonetheless obliged to serve the human community in some other way.

2312 The Church and human reason both assert the permanent validity of the moral law during armed conflict. "The mere fact that war has regrettably broken out does not mean that everything becomes licit between the warring parties."

2313 Non-combatants, wounded soldiers, and prisoners must be respected and treated humanely. Actions deliberately contrary to the law of nations and to its universal principles are crimes, as are the orders that command such actions. Blind obedience does not suffice to excuse those who carry them out. Thus the extermination of a people, nation, or ethnic minority must be condemned as a mortal sin. One is morally bound to resist orders that command genocide.

2315 The accumulation of arms strikes many as a paradoxically suitable way of deterring potential adversaries from war. They see it as the most effective means of ensuring peace among nations. This method of deterrence gives rise to strong moral reservations. The arms race does not ensure peace. Far from eliminating the causes of war, it risks aggravating them. Spending enormous sums to produce ever new types of weapons impedes efforts to aid needy populations; it thwarts the development of peoples. Over-armament multiplies reasons for conflict and increases the danger of escalation.

The legacy of European influence in West Africa

While the teaching of the Catholic Church, as expressed here both in *Gaudium et Spes* and in the *Catechism*, has certainly continued to respond to the changing circumstances of 'armed conflict', which in any case is ever more reliant upon advanced weaponry, it perhaps needs to be reinforced with the earlier caveats of Ambrose and Augustine: combatants themselves are always in danger of succumbing to attitudes that imperil their own humanity (cf. 2312-13 above).

Consider Robert Graves' account (in his memoir *Goodbye to All That*) of how the training of British troops developed in the later stages of WW1:

> *Infantry Training, 1914* laid it down politely that the soldier's ultimate aim was to put out of action or render ineffective the armed forces of the enemy. The War Office no longer [by 1916-17] considered this statement enough for a war of attrition. Troops learned instead that they must HATE the Germans, and KILL as many of them as possible. In bayonet-practice, the men had to make horrible grimaces and utter blood-curdling yells as they charged. The instructors' faces were set in a permanent ghastly grin. 'Hurt him, now! In at the belly! Tear his guts out!' they would scream, as the men charged the dummies ... 'Ruin his chances for life! No more little Fritzes! ... Naoh! Anyone would think that you *loved* the bloody swine!'

According to studies such as D. Grossman's *On Killing*, although humans have natural inhibitions about killing, we have become expert at

desensitising people. While in WW1 shapeless dummies were the target (as for American troops in the picture above), since then the 'enemy' has been depicted more realistically. During the Cold War he was represented as Ivan the Russian, dressed in green with a red star on his helmet. He is now from the Middle East, wearing Arab dress. And since war

has changed, being waged today not on battlefields but mainly in villages and cities, the practice training ground in many countries is a simulated urban location: at Fort Irwin in America, mosques with golden domes can be seen; in Israel a complete ghost town has been built, complete with street signs and named buildings (e.g. The Bank of Palestine, El Baladia City Hall).

However, where military funding is limited, as in Afghanistan, the target may be just a foam mattress with a piece of paper pinned on to it. Paper targets are used in developing countries, and tend to be quite similar, as they are ordered from the same catalogues! There is also much use of the 'virtual' world which can cultivate the 'killer instinct' – now, according to the latest British Army declaration, shared by women as well as men. When Prince Harry served in Afghanistan he told the press that his skill at computer games had helped to prepare him for 'real life' combat. ISIS too uses images from such games on its posters to entice recruits.

If there is one message the Church needs to continue signalling, it is that the person who is actually targeted is a living human being. As Simone Weil expressed it in her *Lectures on Philosophy*:

Human beings are so made that the ones who do the crushing feel nothing; it is the person crushed who feels what is happening. Unless one has placed oneself on the side of the oppressed, to feel with them, one cannot understand.

The heart of Christian teaching about war and its conduct therefore remains the person of Jesus who 'emptied himself, taking the form of a servant, being born in the likeness of men. And being found in human form he humbled himself and became obedient unto death, even death on a cross.'

4. Propaganda and Dissent

'In peace, sons bury their fathers; in war, fathers bury their sons. In peace the sick are healed; in war even the healthy die. In peace there is security in the fields; in war, there is none, not even within city walls.' Those are the words of a poet of an earlier generation. They were spoken by the Orator before his university audience in Cambridge in October 1623, when there were significant calls to launch a new campaign against Spain, not least by the most powerful man in the land, the Duke of Buckingham. They were therefore brave words, whose author's name will be familiar: George Herbert, a rising star whose secular fortunes were put seriously at risk by this speech.

What he perhaps highlights is the abnormality of war, and its dire effects on civilian life. Today we are very conscious that these effects have been vastly heightened by the firepower of modern weaponry, and often last the lifetime of a generation because wars themselves are so prolonged. Those lessons were not apparent to many when the First World War began, although there were sufficient hints in (for example) the Boer wars to indicate how the very nature of war was undergoing radical transformation.

British tactics, little changed from the Crimea, used at Modder River, Magersfontein, Colenso and Spion Kop (shown here) were incapable of winning battles against entrenched troops armed with modern magazine rifles.

Some of the lessons remain to be learnt today. Despite the insistence of Just War thinking that war should only be declared when all diplomatic efforts have been exhausted, leaders of many nations, not least our own, still imagine that military intervention can solve problems more effectively. The rest of us are more aware that

77

ongoing bloodshed, factional fighting and chaos are more likely to be the outcome, as in Iraq, or Libya, or Afghanistan. Our political leaders often speak of 'learning lessons' from governmental mistakes, but there is little evidence that they learn to think through the long-term consequences of their policies.

Nor do they make much attempt to understand what motivates the hostilities that are returned in our direction. The mentality is that of the crusaders back in medieval times. Their supposed objective was to boost the Christian faith, and to resist encroachments against it. Today the Western world, having so very recently discovered the importance of human rights and particular expressions of democracy, believes in propagating these elsewhere – not, let it be noted, by means which are themselves democratic or which respect the lengthy process of debate and decision making which alone can effect lasting change in a country, but by armed intervention (despite the military themselves advising otherwise!). So we repeat the mistakes of the crusaders, and fail to see how much other countries interpret our actions as merely the latest version of imperialism. When resistance mounts, of course we then start to demonise our opponents and our troops are tacitly allowed to perpetrate abuses such as torture or the mass killings of civilians (although these are officially denied for as long as possible). We then wonder why jihadists, whose relatives or forebears may well have suffered as a result of Western policies or involvement, are home-grown in Britain; and why not everyone regards us as quite the civilised nation we imagine ourselves to be. Or perhaps we do not trouble to stand in our opponents' shoes. In a speech given by the senior military adviser to successive American defence secretaries, Marine Lieutenant General John Kelly lumped all extremists together, and said, 'I don't know why they hate us and I don't care ... Our positions can never be reconciled.' And of course, without any attempt to understand 'the other' there can be no reconciliation.

When Prime Ministers here defend sending our troops into action in far-off places that present little or no threat to us, they offer the British public propaganda about defending 'Western values' or 'the British way of life'. 'Universal values' might be a worthier cause, but to speak solely of *our* way of doing things is to drive a wedge between us and them, and makes matters worse. Meanwhile they turn a blind eye to our drug and alcohol addictions, to our pornographic films and magazines, to our devaluation of family life, to our consumerist obsessions, to our celebrity worship, to our dramatically falling church attendances (a symptom of modern secular society) to name but a few – but others notice these things and much prefer their rather different values and their own way of life.

In fact, I have just quoted here what a moderate Imam, who had grown up in Malawi but was then based in Leicester, had to say a few years ago when asked if he could account for the antipathy against British society felt by a good number of Muslims. Tony Blair bears this out more recently in an article he published online last September. From his extensive contacts in the Middle East he now realises:

> We're facing a spectrum of opinion based on a world view which stretches far into parts of Muslim society. At the furthest extreme is the fringe. But at the other end are those who may completely oppose some of the things the fringe does and who would never themselves dream of committing acts of violence, but who unfortunately share certain elements of the fanatic's world view. These elements comprise, *inter alia*: ... a desire to re-shape society according to a set of social and political norms, based on religious belief about Islam, wholly at odds with the way the rest of the world has developed ... a view of the West, particularly the USA, that is innately hostile and regards it essentially as the enemy, not only in policy but in culture and way of living.

What he overlooks here is *firstly* that there are those in Western governments whose aim is certainly to re-shape the world according to a set of social and political norms, based not on any religious beliefs but on contemporary Western ideas which may in many respects clash with the traditions and values of many other countries; and *secondly* that not all Westerners are enamoured of these contemporary mores. Thus, a couple we met in the mid-eighties in South Africa told us they had just returned from spending two years in Britain in an attempt to escape apartheid in their own country. 'We'd been castigated by the West', they said, 'as an evil society and led to believe that Britain was so very different. Indeed it was, but we came back because we concluded that for all its wrongs South Africa was a far more Christian place.' A rather different contrast was drawn at the start of 2015 by the Russian Orthodox Patriarch: he suggested to his flock that their home life compared unfavourably with the ethical standards of many a Muslim household.

Recently I read online a sermon that was preached in Sherborne Abbey on Remembrance Sunday 2008, during the time I was in charge of the Catholic parish there. It was delivered by a distinguished retired major general. He admitted that all was not well in this country: 'Moral standards, decent values, discipline and self-restraint are not always found in many of our homes or our classrooms.' However, he was proud to say that, despite the omni-presence of selfish and consumer-ridden behaviour, the armed forces remained the one hope of the country where commitment and an ethos of service to others was still pre-eminent. Soldiers, he claimed, 'epitomise the very highest qualities of Christian values and human endeavour. Combat strips away the superficialities of life and challenges man to rise above his natural instincts of self-preservation. [War] enables us to pledge ourselves to the service of God and all mankind in the cause of justice and of peace.'

Although I studied his whole address very carefully, I could not discover any reference to soldiers actually being recruited to kill: he seemed to imply that they were merely being asked to go like sheep to the slaughter, like the early Christian martyrs all over again. Had he been honest enough to mention the gruesome prospect of slaughtering others, he might also have explained how 'the natural revulsion against taking life' is deliberately stifled in the process of training; would he then have continued to describe the army in such glowing terms as a school for Christian sanctity? And what about those military personnel who sit in a comfortable air-conditioned cabin far from any scene of action, yet who cause devastation on the ground by firing missiles via a computer screen – hardly even the stuff of heroes, let alone saints? (Even at the start of WW1, D.H.Lawrence, who had seen German troops in action the previous autumn, observed how 'machines' had by then come to dominate the action: 'It is a war of artillery, a war of machines, and men no more than the subjective material of the machine. It is so unnatural as to be unthinkable. Yet we must think of it.')

We shouldn't forget though, that in promoting his military agenda, our major general could no doubt cite considerable ecclesiastical support. At the outset of the 1st World War, the Anglican Bishop of London (Arthur Winnington-Ingram) declared, 'This is a Holy War: we are on the side of Christianity against anti-Christ.' That isn't quite today's rhetoric, which preferred to call the invasion of Iraq 'Operation Iraqi Freedom' and that of Afghanistan 'Operation Enduring Freedom'. If freedom is now a more politically correct objective than the defence of Christianity, that merely tells us that governmental ideologies seldom stay in fashion for any great length of time and continue to change as they often have done in the past. In the 19th century the narrative that justified fighting abroad was that of racial superiority: Charles Darwin saw the extermination of dark-skinned people as an inevitable law of nature, and some British politicians thought it might be a kindness to speed up the process. Hence there were few regrets among the ruling class for 'engineering' a famine in India in 1870s that led to something approaching 10 million deaths. Their ideas unfortunately became influential in Germany, and we know what the so-called 'master' race made of them there. Yet despite putting down Nazism in the 2nd World War we still hung on to racist views of our own long afterwards: we detained and tortured thousands of Kikuyu in Kenya in the 1950s when it suited us. Did our soldiers then 'epitomise the very highest qualities of Christian values', I wonder?

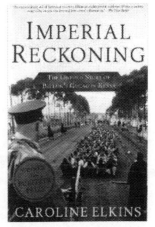

When all else fails, of course the government will plead 'British interests' are at stake, but these tend to be remarkably unstable or inconsistent. In one country we support democrats, in a neighbouring country we turn to despots or dictators. One year we send weapons to an apparently sympathetic faction, but a few years later they turn against us. We deplore the massacre of innocent civilians, but fail to stop the export of the bombs that kill them – after all, it is good for the economy and keeps people in jobs. So when reconsidering Just War theory today we need also to take into account the preparations that are made for war, the size of defence budgets across the world – money which is then not available for health or education or food security, and the vested interests at stake in promoting war. The arms trade may boost our economy and keep people in jobs here, but we should remember that once weapons have left these shores we have precious little control over where they may end up. Perhaps the Dutch people have something to teach us here: Christian-backed campaigns in the Netherlands have over the years been moderately successful in restricting their own arms industry to the needs of self-defence, rather than on exports. They have realised something that we don't seem to appreciate here in Britain, that the arms trade is today one of the root causes of war.

Our situation in Britain as an independent offshore island does mean, I think, that we have stronger *nationalistic* tendencies than some continental countries. There is a marked contrast, for example, between the way we commemorate the past and the German perspective on such matters, which is noticeably more *international*. In a lecture given last year at the British Museum, its Director Andrew MacGregor pointed out that war memorials and commemorations in this country at some level venerate and even celebrate the sacrifices made. Those who died are regarded as latter day saints, and soldiers who engage in fighting today, whether or not it has proper international backing, are termed heroes. We have leaned too far in the direction of jingoism and militarism. We might well recall David Cameron's remarks shortly after becoming Prime Minister: 'I want the armed forces to be at the centre and in the forefront of British life.' My own view, which by now will be obvious, is that they should be in reserve and in the background! Yet in Wye last year we added not one but two new war memorials to the existing stock on display, both of them commemorating those who flew from the local WW1 airfield. One would surely have sufficed? In Germany there are relatively few such memorials, and those that exist are much more likely to be regarded as *mahnmal* (which means a warning monument). MacGregor pointed out that contemporary Germany refuses to see the past in heroic terms and that its exhibitions raise awkward questions about the past. Ours tend not to, and therefore we gain nothing from them to help illuminate the awkward dilemmas of the future. The Professor of International History at Cambridge, David Reynolds, has written, 'The centenary of the Great War is a chance ... to see the conflict in broader terms. It is time not only to remember, but also to understand.'

At this point I want to call upon a number of voices from the past who before, during or after the 1st World War dissented from the official line, insisting that war was not evitable, that it was senseless, that the inhumanity inflicted and the suffering endured was out of all proportion to any good that might have been achieved, and that in any case it was inconclusive (the 2nd World War continued where it left off). There was certainly vociferous opposition in the summer of 1914 to any declaration of war by Britain. The Manchester Guardian (as it then was) argued passionately for British neutrality in a series of editorials. It would be a war 'against England's interests', it would be 'a crime against Europe', it would 'throw away the accumulated progress of half a century'; to enter it would be 'an act of supreme and gratuitous folly'. Even the hawkish Times newspaper remained extremely cautious until 27 July that year, and agreed that on the whole the press had 'avoided taking sides in the quarrel between Austria and Russia'. When two days later the Times commented that 'it is our traditional policy to uphold the balance of power in Europe', the Guardian described this intervention as garrulous, adding that the Times' 'influence at great crises in our foreign affairs has almost always been for evil'. It went on: 'We are friends with every power in Europe. Why give preference to one friend over another?' The next day the editor Charles Scott wrote in a private letter, 'What a monstrous and truly hellish thing this war will be if it really brings the rest of Europe into it.' The leader of 31 July noted what strong influences there were behind the scenes, both social and bureaucratic, 'which are anxious for war ... If the facts were known, and there were free discussion, there would be no danger.' On 3 August it maintained the same stance: This country should not make itself an accessory to the crime against reason and human happiness that is now beginning.' On 4 August it made a final plea: 'we hold it to be the patriotic duty for all good citizens to oppose to the utmost the participation of this country in the greatest crime of our time.'

The predicted 'hellish' scene was soon well in evidence, with thousands of deaths and casualties occurring even in the first month of war. The 'strong influences' behind the scenes had won the day. But, as the historian AJP Taylor observed, neither the cabinet nor parliament actually authorised the declaration of war and the foreign secretary Edward Grey consulted only the Prime Minister Asquith, and 'perhaps not even him', over the decision to send an ultimatum to Germany. One of the factors that by now had to be considered was the pledge that Winston Churchill had made to the French that British ships would defend their channel coast, but again he apparently acted here on his own initiative. So there are serious issues about how such vital decision making should properly be effected in a so-called democracy. The first requirement of a Just War in its traditional expression was to be sanctioned by proper authority. In the British context this surely implies adequate consultation, at least by the elected representatives of the people , even if time is too short to permit as much as the old Roman principle demanded, *Quod omnes tangit, ab omnibus tractari et approbari debet* (what affects everyone should be discussed and approved by all).

It was this sense of millions of working class men being dispatched as cannon fodder to their deaths by the well-heeled upper classes sitting in Whitehall without a 'by your leave' that so angered George Bernard Shaw. At the outbreak of war he ceased writing plays, and published instead a controversial pamphlet, 'Common Sense About the War,' which called Great Britain and its allies equally culpable with the Germans and argued for negotiation and peace. He delivered notorious antiwar speeches which obviously brought him a great deal of criticism. His first play to be performed after the war was *Heartbreak House*, set in a country house just before the war where Shaw exposes the spiritual bankruptcy of the generation responsible for the bloodbath that soon followed. In its Preface he wrote:

> It is said that every people has the Government it deserves. It is more to the point that every Government has the electorate it deserves; for the orators of the front bench can edify or debauch an ignorant electorate at will.

So by then his thinking had moved on: responsibility for the war cannot be laid exclusively upon the country's leadership, however inadequate that may have been; there was a collective failure to engage with the issues as seriously as they demanded.

A protest written by a WW1 conscientious objector

The most prominent among conscientious objectors were those known as the 'Richmond 16', named after one of their places of imprisonment (as in the illustration). They were a disparate group of miners, teachers, clerks, a musician and a footballer, whose consistent refusal, not only to serve in the armed forces but even to be engaged on non-military war work such as stretcher bearing or farm labouring, brought them the severest reprisals including a collective death sentence – which was averted only because their main antagonist Lord Kitchener was blown up by an enemy mine. Although socialist principles were influential in their thinking, they were mostly from non-conformist Christian backgrounds: at one point they were taken to France where their refusal to fight would no longer count as conscientious objection but as desertion, but – in the face of a hostile mob on the quayside at Boulogne – one of their number explained, 'We are just trying to follow the good Saviour', as a result of which the mob drew back respectfully.

In total there were about 16,000 conscientious objectors in WW1, including 1300 so-called 'absolutists' such as the Richmond 16. It was, however, the witness of the latter in 1916 when conscription was being introduced that helped to secure long-lasting protection for the rights of conscience in British law. Tribunals of course had to be persuaded in each individual case, to rule out shirkers or cowards, and much public contempt or abuse was in those days inevitable.

" THIS   LITTLE   PIG   STAYED
AT   HOME "

Opposition to the war was by no means limited to the 'conchies' as they were termed. Whereas they tended to speak as individuals, there had been a growing peace movement in several countries worldwide for a good hundred years. In England the National Peace Council was formed in 1908 soon after the 17th International Peace Congress had taken place (the first one was held in 1843). What, however, brought the movement serious media attention were the voices of prominent public figures such as Mahatma Gandhi, who followed his mentor Leo Tolstoy in advocating non-violent resistance. Likewise in Britain there were influential campaigners for peace such as the philosopher Bertrand Russell. For his pains he ended up in prison and was deprived of his fellowship at Trinity College, Cambridge. (In a satirical essay he suggested that at a time of world crisis the best way forward was for national leaders all to take a break and go to some remote spot quite out of reach of their advisers for at least a month – and do nothing. The world, he thought, would survive quite well without them!)

Above all, though, it was personal experience of the war zone itself which gave rise to much reflection. The first doubts about the wisdom of such colossal expenditure of effort to no apparent end came after a mere four months of fighting, in that famous Christmas Day truce of 1914. Initially its purpose was to fulfilling a dismal task - to bury those whose bodies had been lying in no man's land, some for weeks or months; but then the gesture of respect for each other's dead developed into something more. Both officers and troops crossed the lines and exchanged presents and greetings with their opposite numbers (with a few taking advantage of a rare opportunity to spy out the enemy's position!). There was much mutual agreement that they were 'sick of the war'. More importantly, the enemy was discovered to be a person with whom one could empathise. Left to themselves, the troops that day might have shaken hands and gone home. But wars drag on, since those who commit their troops to commence hostilities seldom have the courage to admit their mistakes. Even after serious reverses or prolonged stalemate the powers that be will insist on continuing the struggle. This in turn guarantees a spate of propaganda which increasingly depicts the enemy in demonic terms and so fuels the hatred.

In later stages of the 1st World War, poets, as well as the artists whom we noted earlier, started to give poignant expression to their war-weariness. It seems to have been the battle of the Somme which triggered this:

DULCE ET DECORUM EST 'A gas poem' of August 1917
Bent double, like old beggars under sacks,
Knock-kneed, coughing like hags, we cursed through sludge,
Till on the haunting flares we turned our backs
And towards our distant rest began to trudge.
Men marched asleep. Many had lost their boots
But limped on, blood-shod. All went lame; all blind;
Drunk with fatigue; deaf even to the hoots
Of tired, outstripped Five-Nines that dropped behind.
Gas! Gas! Quick, boys! — An ecstasy of fumbling,
Fitting the clumsy helmets just in time;
But someone still was yelling out and stumbling,
And flound'ring like a man in fire or lime . .
Dim, through the misty panes and thick green light,

As under a green sea, I saw him drowning.
If in some smothering dreams you too could pace
Behind the wagon that we flung him in,
And watch the white eyes writhing in his face,
His hanging face, like a devil's sick of sin;
If you could hear, at every jolt, the blood
Come gargling from the froth-corrupted lungs,
Obscene as cancer, bitter as the cud
Of vile, incurable sores on innocent tongues, —
My friend, you would not tell with such high zest
To children ardent for some desperate glory,
The old Lie: Dulce et decorum est
Pro patria mori.

Those now famous lines were written by Wilfred Owen, who went down with concussion and trench-fever himself on the Somme, and was later killed in action a week before the Armistice. For many months in 1917 between those pivotal events he was an invalid at Craiglockhart War Hospital on the outskirts of Edinburgh, along with about 100 shell-shocked patients under the care of Dr WHR Rivers (mentioned in chapter 1). Whereas in the day time there was plenty of company, at night the men were on their own; as a fellow officer wrote, each would then become again 'the lonely victim of his dream disaster and delusions'. Owen kept himself as busy and useful as possible, including running a magazine, giving lectures and 'for a quarter of an hour after breakfast' being a poet. He even drafted a full-length play whose aim, he noted, was 'to expose the war to the criticism of reason'. In one letter to his mother, he included what he told her was *important*:

> Send an English Testament to his Grace of Canterbury, and let it consist of that one sentence, at which he winks his eyes:

'Ye have heard that it *hath* been said: An eye for an eye, and a tooth for a tooth: But I say that ye resist not evil, but whosoever shall smite thee on thy right cheek, turn to him the other also.'

And if his reply be 'Most unsuitable for the present distressing moment, my dear lady! But I trust that in God's good time ... etc.' – *then there is only one possible conclusion*, that there are no more Christians at the present moment than there were at the end of the first century.

It was just at this time that he became acquainted in the hospital with another more recent patient, Siegfried Sassoon, another of the Great War poets. Like Owen, Sassoon had seen active service at the Somme, and indeed had gained the M.C. for his 'Mad Jack' bravery in rescuing a wounded colleague in the most dangerous of circumstances. Not long afterwards he was back in England where (after meeting several prominent pacifists such as Bertrand Russell) he courageously made public the strongly-worded protest he had already addressed to his commanding officer:

I am making this statement as an act of wilful defiance of military authority, because I believe that the war is being deliberately prolonged by those who have the power to end it.

I am a soldier, convinced that I am acting on behalf of soldiers. I believe that this war, upon which I entered as a war of defence and liberation, has now become a war of aggression and conquest. I believe that the purposes for which I and my fellow-soldiers entered upon this war should have been so clearly stated as to have made it impossible to change them, and that, had this been done, the objects which actuated us would now be attainable by negotiation.

I have seen and endured the sufferings of the troops, and I can no longer be a party to prolong these sufferings for ends which I believe to be evil and unjust.

I am not protesting against the conduct of the war, but against the political errors and insincerities for which the fighting men are being sacrificed.

On behalf of those who are suffering now I make this protest against the deception which is being practised on them; also I believe that I may help to destroy the callous complacence with which the majority of those at home regard the continuance of agonies which they do not share, and which they have not sufficient imagination to realize.

July, 1917 S. Sassoon

Although this public statement resulted in a question asked in the House of Commons, Sassoon's friend Robert Graves considered it a futile gesture bound to place heavier burdens upon him. He campaigned with the military authorities to prevent Sassoon being made a martyr to what – at that stage of the war – was evidently a lost cause, and the War Office quickly arranged for his admittance to Craiglockhart as one in urgent need of medical attention.

Once there he and Owen soon found that they had a great deal in common. In particular, one of Sassoon's poems already published in *The Old Huntsman* resonates strongly with Owen's remarks (quoted above) to his mother:

`THEY'

The Bishop tells us: 'When the boys come back
They will not be the same; for they'll have fought
In a just cause; they lead the last attack
On Anti-Christ; their comrades' blood has bought
New right to breed an honourable race.
They have challenged Death and dared him face to face.'
'We're none of us the same!' the boys reply.
'For George lost both his legs; and Bill's stone blind;
Poor Jim's shot through the lungs and like to die;
And Bert's gone syphilitic: you'll not find

90

A chap who's served that hasn't found some change.'
And the Bishop said: 'The ways of God are strange!'

Apart from these two leading war poets there were others such as AE Housman and Ivor Gurney. In time several of their poems received musical settings, and so reached a wider audience. Much later some of Owen's poems were used by Benjamin Britten in his *War Requiem*, which continues to be one of the most powerful witnesses to the tragedies of war and the truths that can yet emerge from it. Collectively these poems offer a counter-narrative to 'the old lie', the jingoism and militarism that resurface all too easily in British society. They express variously anger, sadness, compassion, and a sense of shared humanity. The most moving for me is the one I studied for O level well over fifty years ago – written once again by Wilfred Owen:

> STRANGE MEETING
> It seemed that out of battle I escaped
> Down some profound dull tunnel, long since scooped
> Through granites which titanic wars had groined.
> Yet also there encumbered sleepers groaned,
> Too fast in thought or death to be bestirred.
> Then, as I probed them, one sprang up, and stared
> With piteous recognition in fixed eyes,
> Lifting distressful hands as if to bless.
> And by his smile, I knew that sullen hall,
> By his dead smile I knew we stood in Hell.
> With a thousand pains that vision's face was grained;
> Yet no blood reached there from the upper ground,
> And no guns thumped, or down the flues made moan.
> "Strange friend," I said, "here is no cause to mourn."
> "None," said that other, "save the undone years,
> The hopelessness. Whatever hope is yours,
> Was my life also; I went hunting wild
> After the wildest beauty in the world,
> Which lies not calm in eyes, or braided hair,
> But mocks the steady running of the hour,
> And if it grieves, grieves richlier than here.

For of my glee might many men have laughed,
And of my weeping something had been left,
Which must die now. I mean the truth untold,
The pity of war, the pity war distilled.
Now men will go content with what we spoiled,
Or, discontent, boil bloody, and be spilled.
They will be swift with swiftness of the tigress.
None will break ranks, though nations trek from progress.
Courage was mine, and I had mystery,
Wisdom was mine, and I had mastery:
To miss the march of this retreating world
Into vain citadels that are not walled.
Then, when much blood had clogged their chariot-wheels,
I would go up and wash them from sweet wells,
Even with truths that lie too deep for taint.
I would have poured my spirit without stint
But not through wounds; not on the cess of war.
Foreheads of men have bled where no wounds were.
I am the enemy you killed, my friend.
I knew you in this dark: for so you frowned
Yesterday through me as you jabbed and killed.
I parried; but my hands were loathe and cold.
Let us sleep now . . . ."

These war poets were predominantly drawn from the ranks of well-educated officers; so it is worth hearing testimony from 'other ranks' as well. Here I call upon a recently deceased veteran who was known personally to Sarah (my wife) in her early teenage years. She lived just south of Bath in Combe Down, where her father was for many years the vicar. Combe Down was also the place where the renowned Harry Patch was born, and after the 2nd World War he was still living there  and working mainly as a plumber. Sarah remembers him as a kind, gentle man whose hair in his mid 50s had already turned white. He was very generous in the time he gave to the Vicarage, where he redecorated it throughout for her parents. After he had turned 100 (in 1998) he was sought out by the media for his reminiscences of the 1st World War, being one of the few surviving soldiers who had fought in the trenches. It seems unlikely that they expected to hear comments as critical as those Mr Patch offered them. He reflected on his lost friends and the moment when  he himself first came face to face with a German soldier. He recalled at that moment, he said, the story of Moses descending from Mount Sinai with God's Ten Commandments. He remembered the divine command 'Thou shalt not kill', and found himself unable to shoot his opposite number dead, despite having the opportunity to do so. Instead he wounded and disabled him. Subsequently he described war as the 'calculated and condoned slaughter of human beings', which, he added, was not worth taking even a single life. 'War is organised murder', was his conclusion. 'I felt then, as I feel now, that the politicians who took us to war should have been given the guns and told to settle their differences themselves, instead of organising nothing better than legalised mass murder.'

A century ago (as indicated earlier) there were certainly peace movements in a number of countries, but they were then less well-supported than their equivalents are today. The main such Catholic organisation is Pax Christi, whose rationale is that recourse to violence has historically been far less common than the resolution of problems by non-violent means whose aim is to convert the oppressor, not to conquer him. The outcome is not therefore to be described crudely as 'victory' (nor its opposite, 'defeat'), but rather as a negotiated transformation of political attitudes and public consciousness. More often than not, great persistence is needed involving many small steps over a long period of time. The danger of a militaristic approach, by contrast, is that it hopes that a fiercely aggressive response will bring about rapid change. Yet even if it seems to succeed, the change may well not last for long given the reality that in an ever-changing world unforeseen consequences can quickly mount up.

In an epoch when results are expected rapidly, the paths of non-violence and patient diplomacy are sadly not likely to be very popular with those who have achieved positions of power and authority. Yet experienced international players know that realistic aims are generally those in which all parties feel they have gained sufficient to compensate any concessions they may have made — and that to reach such a point requires a great deal of unhurried negotiation.

The two reflections that follow are therefore of profound relevance to the present age. The first comes from ancient sources, probably from the Greek epoch already highlighted. Aesop is believed to be a slave who knew many of the wise fables that now bear his name. Various Greek authors refer to him — Herodotus suggests that he won his freedom by telling such stories. The evidence now is that some of them go back much further; for example, there are Sumerian fables remarkably similar to some of his that were discovered on cuneiform tablets dated to around 1800 BC. The Aesop fable that bears on our theme tells of the competition between the Wind and the Sun.

The Wind and the Sun were disputing which was the stronger. Suddenly they saw a traveller coming down the road, and the Sun said: 'I see a way to decide our dispute. Whichever of us can cause that traveller to take off his cloak shall be regarded as the stronger. You begin.' So the Sun retired behind a cloud, and the Wind began to blow as hard as it could upon the traveller. But the harder he blew the more closely did the traveller wrap his cloak round him, till at last the Wind had to give up in despair. Then the Sun came out and shone in all  his glory upon the traveller, who soon found it too hot to walk with his cloak on.

The second reflection is from a much more recent spiritual source with strong local connections. Simone Weil died at the age of 34 in August

1943 in Ashford, where she is buried in Bybrook Cemetery. The dual carriageway that gives access to various shopping precincts is named after her; her writings, on the other hand, open

up profound avenues for thought! During the 1st World War she heard that soldiers were unable to get hold of sugar rations, so at the age of 6 she practised self-denial and gave up eating sugar herself. During the 2nd World War she limited her food intake to what she believed residents ate in the parts of France under German occupation. Very likely she ate even less, as it is recorded that she refused food on most occasions. It was in the sanatorium in Ashford (where several Free French were also cared for) that one of our present congregation at St Ambrose' Church, then

> What a country calls its vital... interests are not things that help its people live, but things that help it make war.

assisting the matron, was present when a rabbi (her family was Jewish) came to embalm her. After she died the coroner's report said: 'The deceased did kill and slay herself by refusing to eat whilst the balance of her mind was disturbed'.

Perhaps, however, her desire to express some form of solidarity with the victims of the war was not 'insanity', but an act of love. It certainly coheres with what she wrote in her most famous book *Waiting for God*, where she described God's own self-renunciation:

> The religions which have a conception of this renunciation, this voluntary distance, this voluntary self-effacement of God, his apparent absence and his secret presence here below, these religions are true religions, the translation into different languages of the great Revelation. The religions which represent divinity as commanding wherever it has the power to do so are false.

God is not, in other words, a cosmic commander whose will is to be enforced by those who adhere to such a belief. The Bishop of London was wrong when he described the 1st World War as a Holy War and both

95

Deuteronomy and the Qur'an were wrong to portray God's purpose as the extermination of his supposed enemies. A Just War may still be justified if all peaceful means of resistance have genuinely been exhausted, but a Holy War – never. The Cross of Christ is clear testimony that such is not God's way.

* * * * * * * * *

Tragically though, wholesale slaughter continues apace in the modern world and a host of reasons are still too easily found to justify it. As Wilfred Owen – reflecting on the biblical story of Abraham and Isaac, in which Isaac's life was dramatically spared – wrote in *The Parable of the Old Man and the Young*, a poem later set to music by Benjamin Britten in his *War Requiem*:

The old man would not so, but slew his son,

And half the seed of Europe, one by one.

God prevents the sacrifice of Isaac
(13th/14th century Holland Psalter, at St John's College, Cambridge)

Printed in the United States
By Bookmasters